Understanding Your Employee Benefits

From Enrollment to Claims: A Comprehensive
Guide to Navigating Your Employee Benefits

Howard E. Deihl, RHU

Published by Howard E. Deihl, RHU

4400 State Hwy 121, Suite 300
Lewisville, TX 75056

www.thegeneralagency.com

Deihl, Howard E., RHU

Title: Understanding Your Employee Benefits
           Employees Guide to Benefits

ISBN: 9798862103236

Imprint: Independently published

The materials contained in this publication represent the opinion of the author and editor and should not be construed to be a view or opinions of the companies with whom such persons are or may be in partnership with, associated with, or employed by.

Always consult with a licensed agent, attorney, accountant, and tax professional when making decisions related to employee benefits.

Printed in the United States of America

Cover design by Howard E. Deihl, RHU

10 9 8 7 6 5 4 3 2 1

Table of Contents

Chapter 5

Chapter 6

Chapter 7

Chapter 8

Chapter 9

Chapter 10

Chapter 11

Chapter 12

Chapter 13

Chapter 14

Chapter 1

Introduction to Employee Benefits

In today's work environment, employee benefits have emerged as more than just added perks. They are essential components that complement our salaries and significantly influence our overall job satisfaction. This book serves as a guide to making the most of your benefits and making good choices.

We will also explore numerous benefits that you may be entitled to and the importance of each one. I will also demonstrate how do they work, and answer these questions: Why are they offered? How do they enhance your overall compensation? And more.

As you know, one size rarely fits all, especially when it comes to benefit plans. Whether you are single, married, or have a growing family, your employer may offer an ideal plan for you. Here, I will walk you through the steps and considerations to keep in mind when selecting the plan that aligns best with your circumstances.

Claims can also be a difficult challenge when dealing with your benefits. And this book, I will also break down the claims process into easy-to-understand segments, highlighting common issues people face and providing solutions.

As we know, life is full of surprises, some planned and others unexpected. From welcoming a new child to changes in marital status, these events can significantly impact how you approach and use your benefits. By taking proactive steps you can make informative decisions during these transformative life phases.

In this book, I will share real-life scenarios that illustrate the application of benefit rules, demonstrate the premium calculation processes, and guide you in optimizing your benefits efficiently.

As your career progresses, it is vital to be well-equipped with the knowledge and tools to maximize the advantages of your employment. Consider this book a valuable resource, ready to assist and guide you at every twist and turn of your professional journey.

I understand insurance books are not exactly thrilling reads, however I will aim to make it as entertaining as possible while still highlighting the importance of your benefits. I will also include "call-outs", "takeaways" and real-life scenarios for better retention.

Chapter 2

Enrollment: Being Part of a Group Enrollment

"Don't be that guy *(or Girl)*** !**

When a group is enrolling for the first time, or changing insurance companies, it is often necessary for <u>every</u> employee in the business to complete applications. "That guy" is the one who takes his application home to his or her spouse and either never returns it or returns it late. This delays the enrollment process for the entire business. Everyone understands the importance of including spouses and significant others in these important decisions.

A few common ways to avoid application delays are:

- Calling your spouse, significant other or primary care-giver on the phone during the enrollment process.

- Having them on speakerphone during enrollment meetings.

- Inviting them to the benefit meetings if the employer permits.

This scenario <u>only</u> applies when your company is changing insurance companies and the entire group must enroll at the same time. This does not apply to new hires or employees in an "individual open enrollment" or "special open enrollment". I will cover individual open enrollment and special enrollments later in this chapter.

Enrollment Processes

When your employer changes insurance companies, there are basically three types of enrollment processes:

1. **Electronic enrollment:** This is when your company sends you a link to either your phone or your computer and allows you to enroll electronically. These are typically handled by third-party enrollment platforms. With the electronic enrollment process, you answer the questions and submit your information. Additionally, the electronic enrollment software company sends reports to your employer and gives them a status of how many employees have enrolled and who is outstanding.

2. **Paper applications <u>without</u> medical questions:** These applications are generally very simple. They typically only ask you to include your name, address, date of birth, date of hire, and a list of your dependents if you

are enrolling them. If you are enrolling your dependents, you will need to include their date of birth, social security numbers, and in some cases, their address if you have children off at college or dependents that reside with a former spouse.

3. **Paper applications with medical questions:** When you are asked to complete an application with medical questions, you may want to keep your information private and not disclose this with your employer. In this scenario, you can place your completed application in a sealed envelope and ask that it be submitted directly to the insurance company underwriter to ensure your privacy.

IMPORTANT NOTE: When answering medical questions on an application, be sure to read it carefully. If the insurance company is asking for your medical history for the past five years and you include medical conditions from 10 years ago, the insurance company will underwrite for it and may increase your premiums.

For example, if you had a heart attack 10 years ago, but the application is only asking for medical conditions within the past five years, the underwriter can add additional points for the heart attack. However, if you are currently taking medications for a condition that happened 10 years ago, you must include this on the application.

Remember, prompt enrollment plays a crucial role. Your employer is responsible for an accurate headcount to avoid discrimination and participation rules. Every day your application is not returned is another day of delay in receiving approval and receiving benefit ID cards.

Be considerate! You may not need to use your benefits right away, but you may have coworkers with scheduled doctor's appointments for themselves or their families who desperately need their coverage. Don't be "that guy"!

If You Are Waiving or Denying Coverage

If you are choosing to waive coverage, you are still required to complete the enrollment process. As I mentioned before, your employer is required to account for everyone in the company. On the applications or enrollment platform, there is a waiver section and the reason for waiving group coverage.

Here are some of the common reasons for waiving coverage, and it is important to understand the implications:

- I have other group coverage. For example, coverage on a spouse's plan.

- I have Medicare.

- I have Medicaid.

- I have an individual health insurance plan.

- I am not enrolled in a health insurance plan, and I do not want coverage.

The last reason is very important! If you waive coverage and do not have coverage elsewhere, you will not be able to enroll until your company's next open enrollment period or you have a qualifying event. This means if you are healthy now and choose to go without coverage, and you are suddenly diagnosed with an illness or have an accident, you will not be covered. This may sound like common sense, but there have been employees in the past who tried to jump onto the group health plan when these situations occurred.

In addition, your reason for waiving coverage can have an impact on your employer's participation requirements. Most insurance companies have participation requirements that must be met for your employer to qualify for group benefits.

Here is a real-life example.

During a company benefit enrollment meeting, a few employees decided to waive coverage because they did not want $23 taken out of their check. One of these employees convinced a coworker to waive coverage also. A few months later that coworker was involved in a motorcycle accident and accumulated over $100,000 in medical expenses. Needless to say, the employee that convinced his coworker to waive coverage has felt guilty ever since. Do not put yourself in this situation.

Do Not Influence Others

Each employee's budget, salary, needs, and medical conditions are unique to each person. Helping a coworker decide between plan designs or whether or not to take coverage may sound like a noble gesture, however, it is best to refer them to an insurance professional.

Garbage In, Garbage Out

When enrolling in your group health plan, remember to write legibly and provide accurate information. This statement may sound ridiculous, but it can save you trouble in the long run.

- **Illegible names on your application:** Unreadable or misspelled names can result in your claims initially being denied by the insurance company. This is not the insurance company being the "bad guy"; your claims are typically denied due to a data mismatch. In addition, you will need to go through the process of ordering a corrected ID card, which can be avoided on the front end.

- **Incorrect date of hire:** If your employer has a waiting period on a group health plan, you may be put into the waiting period even though you started employment prior to the waiting period window.

- **Incorrect Social Security numbers or dates of birth on yourself or your dependents:** This can also result in your claims being initially denied due to a data mismatch.

- **Incorrect or illegible addresses:** Incorrect addresses are the main reasons for lost or mis-delivered ID cards.

This might sound like common sense; however, it happens frequently.

Employment Applications vs. Employee Benefit Applications

As previously mentioned in this chapter, many times you may be asked to enroll with an electronic enrollment platform. These enrollment platforms receive data from your employer which may be out of date since your date of hire. Many times, your employer sends a spreadsheet or a data transfer to your broker or insurance company. If this information is not kept up to date, or your employment application when you were initially hired was illegible or incorrect, it can result in your claims being initially denied or a loss of your ID cards.

Additionally, these enrollment platforms commonly communicate with you via SMS or e-mail addresses. So, it is important to remember to keep the information your employer has on file up to date.

Steps to Ensure Timely Enrollment

1. Know your deadline.

2. Gather all the required information ahead of time.

3. Address any questions you may have sooner rather than later.

4. If you have someone you need to discuss your plan choices with, do it promptly.

5. Once you have all of the information, submit your application.

The enrollment process is not just about filling out a form. This process affects your employer, you, and your coworkers. Always remember to take the process seriously, be thorough, and always start on the right foot.

Chapter 3

Enrollment for New Hires and Employees Not Currently Enrolled

When you join a new company, understanding when and how you can enroll in the group health plan is crucial. This chapter will guide both new and existing employees who might have waived coverage through the process, ensuring seamless integration into the group health plan.

Enrollment Period for New Hires

Some employers offer immediate enrollment for new hires. This means that as soon as the employee begins their first day, they are eligible to join the group health plan. However, many employers have a standard period post-hire before an employee can enroll. This is typically 30 to 60 days from the date of hire. Under the Affordable Care Act (ACA), the maximum allowed waiting period is 90 days. This means that employers cannot require employees to wait more than three months after their hire date before offering health coverage. The waiting period is a period of time between the date of hire and when an employee is eligible to enroll in the employer-sponsored health plan. It is worth noting that a waiting period is different than probationary period that the employer might have.

Submission Deadlines to the Insurance Company

Once you enroll in the health plan, it is the responsibility of the employer to submit this enrollment information to the insurance company. Most insurance companies require enrollment within the waiting period.

Along with the enrollment form, your employer might need to provide supporting documents such as proof of eligibility (e.g., employment contract, or payroll report). In the rare case that an employer fails to submit an application on time there can be a range of consequences such as coverage delays, administrative challenges, and possibly legal consequences.

Do not exceed your waiting period!

When completing your enrollment form, ensure you fill it out clearly and accurately. Proper documentation will help avoid future complications, like ID cards lost in the mail or claims issues when you are trying to use your benefits. Insurance providers rely on the information you provide, and discrepancies in their system can lead to denied claims.

Consequences of Waiving Off a Group Health Plan

Choosing to waive off a group health plan can have both immediate and long-term repercussions. Initially, one might benefit from an increased take-home salary, as some employers offer cash incentives or wage adjustments for those not taking advantage of the group plan. However, without this employer-sponsored coverage, an individual might need to seek personal health insurance which can be considerably more expensive and might not offer comparable benefits. Moreover, personal plans can have restrictions based on pre-existing conditions, unlike

If you waive coverage you will need to wait until open enrollment, have a qualifying event to enroll.

many group plans. In the event of a medical emergency or the onset of a chronic illness, the financial burden without the safety net of a group health plan can be significant. Furthermore, waiving off might mean missing out on preventive care benefits, leading to potential health issues down the road. Additionally, rejoining a group plan after waiving it might come with waiting periods or restrictions. Thus, while there might be immediate financial advantages, the risks associated with forgoing this coverage should be weighed carefully.

When Can Current Employees Join a Group Plan?

If you are an existing employee who has not signed up for your company's health plan, you only have   two primary opportunities to do so. You will need to wait for the open enrollment period or if you have a qualifying event you can take advantage of Special Enrollment Periods (SEP). Understanding the distinction between these two periods is crucial.

Open Enrollment VS. Special Enrollment Period

Open Enrollment: Open enrollment is a designated period, typically occurring once a year, during which members of a group health insurance plan can make changes to their coverage. It allows employees and members (such as COBRA and State Continuation participants) the opportunity to review their current coverage and make any necessary changes for the upcoming year. This might include enrolling in a plan for the first time, changing plans, adding, or removing dependents, or declining coverage.

The exact dates of open enrollment can vary by employer or insurance carrier, but it's generally a set timeframe. For example, many employer-sponsored plans have open enrollment in the fall for coverage that starts at renewal on January 1st of the following year. If your employer has a renewal date other than January 1st, your open enrollment date will be 30 days prior to the renewal date.

Qualifying Event Open Enrollment (often called Special Enrollment Periods or SEPs): This is a period of time outside of the regular open enrollment period during which individuals can enroll in or change their health insurance coverage due to certain life events. Events such as getting married, having a baby, losing other health coverage, or moving to a new residence might change an individual's insurance needs. The SEP is designed to allow individuals to adjust their coverage in response to these major life changes.

Here is a more comprehensive list of qualifying life events commonly recognized:

- Marriage

- Divorce or legal separation (which results in loss of health insurance)

- Death of a spouse (leading to loss of coverage)

- Birth of a child

- Adoption of a child or placement for adoption

- Foster care placement

- Death of a covered member of the household

- Losing eligibility for job-based coverage (for reasons such as quitting, being laid off, or reductions in hours worked)

- Loss of individual health coverage for a plan or policy you bought yourself

- Losing eligibility for Medicaid or CHIP (Children's Health Insurance Program)

- Aging off a parent's plan (typically occurs at age 26)

- Expiration of COBRA coverage

- Loss of retiree coverage

- Moving to a new home in a new ZIP code or county

- Moving to a new state

- Moving to or from the place you attend school (as a student)

- Gaining citizenship or lawful presence in the U.S.

- Release from jail or prison

- Becoming ineligible for Medicaid due to a change in income

Remember, after experiencing a qualifying life event, there is typically a limited timeframe (usually 30 to 60 days) during which one can make changes to their insurance or enroll in a new plan. If you do not act within this window, you may have to wait until the next open enrollment period to make changes. If you have questions regarding open enrollment periods, consult with your employer, HR department or your employer's insurance broker for more information.

Chapter 4

Health Insurance Plan Types

Health insurance protects you from the financial implications of unexpected health events. By choosing the right plan, you can protect yourself from soaring medical expenses while also ensuring you and your family receive quality care. This chapter explains the various types of medical insurance, how to select the right plan, and how to calculate the potential costs involved.

Is this plan offered **Health Maintenance Organization (HMO)**

HMO plans require members to select a primary care physician (PCP). To see a specialist, members generally need a referral from their PCP. HMO plans typically offer lower premiums and lower out-of-pocket costs. While some people are not fans of HMOs due to network restrictions, this structure has its advantages. With an HMO, there is less chance you will receive unexpected bills from out-of-network providers during a hospital stay. For instance, with a PPO, even if you visit an in-network hospital, you might still be treated by out-of-network specialists, like an anesthesiologist or radiologist. This can lead to higher costs for you. For the most part, HMOs largely prevent such surprises. Plus, HMO plans often come with patient advocates who help ensure you see in-network providers. Remember, HMO plan can also cover your world-wide for emergencies and accidents. If something happens to you abroad, just call your insurance company for directions. Also request your medical bills are in English and American currency.

Is this plan offered ☑ ☐ **Preferred Provider Organization (PPO)**

PPO plans give you freedom and flexibility when you are seeking medical care. With a PPO, you do not need a referral to see any doctor, whether it is your primary care doctor or a specialist. Plus, you can choose doctors outside of the plan's network. But there's a trade-off. This flexibility often means you could pay higher premiums and have more out-of-pocket cost. With PPOs, the costs can differ when you see use in-network or out-of-network doctors, with separate de-ductibles, coinsurance, and out-of-pocket limits for each. Some PPOs even have no maximum limit for out-of-network services, meaning the insurance company might cover only 60% of your bills indefinitely. However, a silver lining is that many PPOs have extensive nationwide networks, making it simple to find in-network hospitals and doctors.

Is this plan offered ☑ ☐ Exclusive Provider Organization (EPO)

Exclusive Provider Organizations (EPOs) blend elements of HMO and PPO plans. Like an HMO, EPOs generally will not cover treatment from out of network doctors or hospitals. However, they differ in a significant way: you do not need a referral from a primary care doctor to see a specialist within the network, offering more flexibility than an HMO. In addition, an EPO will cover out-of-network costs during emergencies. So, if you face a pressing medical issue, on most plans you can receive coverage even if you are treated outside its designated network.

Is this plan offered ☑ ☐ Point-of-Service (POS)

Point of Service (POS) plans blend features from both PPO and HMO models. Essentially, they are built on an HMO foundation but with added flexibility. Like an HMO, you will need a referral from your primary care doctor to see a specialist. However, unlike strict HMOs, POS plans let you venture outside their network for care. But use caution. If you do choose to go outside the network, you will most likely encounter a separate deductible and separate coinsurance, meaning you might pay more. In essence, POS plans offer a middle ground, granting more freedom than traditional HMOs by allowing out-of-network options.

Is this plan offered ☑ ☐ ## Reference-Based Pricing

Reference-Based Pricing (RBP) is another option for those exploring health insurance. In simple terms, with RBP, insurance does not pay based on pre-set prices with hospitals or doctors. Instead, it pays based on a set Medicare benchmark. This can make healthcare costs more transparent and more affordable. However, people with RBP plans often run into medical claims more frequently. Later in this book, I will provide guidance on how to avoid many of these claim challenges. While RBP offers more clarity on costs, it is essential to understand the details and its potential downsides before choosing this plan.

Is this plan offered ☑ ☐ ## Catastrophic Health Insurance

Catastrophic health insurance plans are tailored mainly for younger individuals, specifically those under 30, or others who meet certain criteria due to financial hardships or other challenges. The primary characteristic of these plans is their high deductibles, meaning the amount you would pay out-of-pocket before insurance starts covering. On the bright side, while the upfront costs might be steep in case of medical events, the monthly premiums (or the regular fee you pay to keep the insurance) are relatively low. This balance makes them a viable choice for those who want to keep their recurring insurance costs minimal but are prepared for higher costs if significant medical care is needed.

Is this plan offered ✓ ☐ **High Deductible Health Plans (HDHP)**

High Deductible Health Plans, often referred to as HDHPs, are typically paired with Health Savings Accounts (HSAs). These plans come with higher deductibles, which meet they IRS minimum standards for tax exemption meaning you must meet your deductible for all services except preventive services before your insurance starts paying. Many people choose these plans for the tax advantages. The money you use for the deductible is tax-free, allowing you to set up an HSA, a special savings account for medical expenses. Many HDHPs operate similarly to PPOs, giving you a network of preferred healthcare providers and letting you choose outside providers as well. This approach offers a blend of potential long-term savings, tax benefits, and upfront healthcare costs.

If you have an HSA, you cannot use it to cover expenses for family members (or others) who do not have a High Deductible Heath Plan.

If you are enrolled in an HDHP and have a Health Savings Account (HSA), you can you use tax-free dollars for services like vision and dental care. So if you have eye exams, glasses, dental cleanings, or fillings, you can use your HSA funds tax free. Additionally, if there are any costs your vision or dental insurance does not cover, like coinsurance fees, your HSA can step in to help cover those expenses as well. This provides a versatile and tax-efficient way to manage healthcare expenses

If you are enrolled in a high-deductible health plan (HDHP). You can make tax-free withdrawals from your HSA bank account to pay for qualified medical expenses. The exact list of qualified medical expenses can be found in IRS Publication 502, but here is an overview of common items and services: across the board.

- Doctor visits

- Surgeries

- Lab tests

- X-rays

- Prescription medications

- Pain relievers (with a rescription)

- Cold and flu medicine (with a prescription)

- Allergy medicine (with a prescription)

- Crutches

- Bandages

- Blood sugar test kits for Diabetics

- Hearing aids and batteries

- Eyeglasses

- Contact lenses and solution

- Eye exams

- Eye surgeries like LASIK

- Dental cleanings

- Dental Fillings

- Orthodontics (braces)

- Dental Extractions

- Mental Health Counseling

- Psychotherapy

- Psychiatric care

- Chiropractic care

- Physical therapy

- Long-term care services

- Substance abuse treatments

- Birth control pills and devices

- Prenatal vitamins

- Birth classes

- Delivery and postnatal care

- Occupational therapy

- Speech therapy

- Health screenings and preventive services

- Wheelchairs and maintenance

It is important to keep your receipts and documentation for any medical expenses you pay for using your HSA. Remember the IRS can up-date the list of qualified expenses or provide additional clarifications over time. Non-qualified withdrawals from your HSA will be subject to taxes and, if you are under 65, you will be subject to an additional 20% penalty.

DO NOT use your HSA bank card to pay for non-approved items.

Some items or services might need a Letter of Medical Necessity (LMN) from your healthcare provider to be consid-ered a qualified expense. Always consult with a tax advisor or review the most recent IRS Publication 502 for the definitive list of qualified medical expenses.

Chapter 5

Choosing the Plan That is Right for You

When it comes to health insurance, there is no one-size-fits-all answer. The perfect plan for your friend or colleague may not be right for you. This chapter will guide you on which questions to ask. Don't forget to jot down notes!

Step 1: Assess Your Needs

- **Health Conditions:** Begin by evaluating your current health status. Do you have any pre-existing conditions? Are you generally in good health and rarely see a doctor, or do you frequently require medical attention?

- **Specialists and Doctor Visits:** If you regularly see specialists or have appointments often, you will want a plan that covers these needs without causing financial strain.

- **Network Providers and Hospitals:** Many people have preferred doctors, hospitals and specialists. If you are one of them, you will want to ensure your doctor is included in the insurance plan's network.

Step 2: Consider Your Budget

- **Monthly Premium:** This is the amount you pay monthly, regardless of whether you use medical services or not. It is essential to find a premium you can comfortably afford.

- **Deductibles:** This is the amount you pay out of pocket before your insurance begins to cover costs. If you have a high deductible, you will pay more upfront whe you use the coverage, but generally, your monthly premium will be lower (and vice versa).

- **Copays:** On most plans when you visit a doctor, get a prescription, or use a health service, you might need to make a small payment called a copay. In some cases, for more urgent care, or hospital admissions, these co-payments can be higher.

- **Maximum Out-of-Pocket:** This is the most you'd pay during a calendar year for covered health services. Once you've reached this amount, the insurance will typically cover 100% of the costs for covered benefits. Make sure this amount is something you'd be able to handle in case of a medical emergency.

Step 3: Evaluate Additional Benefits

- **Flexible Spending Accounts (FSAs):** Some employers offer these accounts which allow you to set aside money from your paycheck before taxes to pay for out-of-pocket healthcare costs.

- **Gap Plans:** Gap health insurance provides benefits that your primary health insurance might not cover. These can include benefits for hospital stays or specific diseases.

Step 4: Attend Benefits Meetings

If your employer is offering a health benefits meeting, it's wise to attend. Bring along anyone who plays a significant role in your healthcare decisions, such as a spouse or primary caregiver for dependents.

Step 5: Prepare Your Questions

Go into any meetings or discussions armed with questions. Whether you're talking to a broker, company representative, or your employer, it's crucial to fully understand the plans available to you.

Some sample questions might include:

- Is my regular doctor in this plan's network?

- How much will I pay for specialist visits?

- Are my medications covered under this plan?

- What happens if I need emergency care out of the network?

- Are there any additional benefits, like vision or dental?

Selecting the right health plan is an important decision that can significantly impact both your physical and financial well-being. With careful consideration and a thorough understanding of your options, you can find a plan that serves your unique needs. Remember, the best health plan for you is the one that aligns with your medical needs and budget.

Calculating Cost

Many employers offer multiple health plans to choose from. If your employer offers more than one plan design, it is important to consider the following key financial factors when making your choice:

1. **Cost Per Pay Period:** The term "Monthly Premium" is the amount you pay each month for your health insurance, whether you use medical services or not. This refers to the regular amount deducted from your

paycheck for the insurance coverage. Balancing this cost against your budget is crucial in determining the plan's affordability.

2. **Maximum Out-of-Pocket Cost:** This is the upper limit you would be responsible for paying during a policy period. Once this threshold is reached, the insurance covers 100% of the subsequent expenses. Keep in mind, on many group health insurance plans, co-payments for doctor visits and sometimes even prescription drugs can contribute to your out-of-pocket maximum. This is especially true for metallic plans under the Affordable Care Act. It is highly recommended to check with your broker or plan administrator to see if co-payments count towards your maximum out-of-pocket limit.

Take this into consideration: if significant health events, like a pregnancy or surgery, are on the horizon, it may be more economical to pay a slightly higher insurance premium now to mitigate hefty costs down the line. Balancing these two factors will help you choose a plan that combines affordability with comprehensive protection.

Here is an example of a cost calculation comparing to plan designs. Consider this example:
An employer is offering 2 HMO Plans.

"Plan A" is an HMO with a $3,000 deductible, which costs an employee $43.84 per pay period. This employee has 26 pay periods in a year, so the total annual cost for "Plan A" comes to $1,139.84. The maximum out-of-pocket expense for this plan is $8,700 annually.

On the other hand, "Plan B" costs $90.41 per pay period, which is an annual cost of $2,350.66. Although this employee would pay $1,210.82 more for "Plan B" each year, the maximum out-of-pocket expense is significantly lower at $1,500 annually. This means the potential maximum out-of-pocket savings is $7,200 with Plan B.

Selecting the appropriate health insurance plan requires understanding the various plan types and conducting a thorough assessment of personal health needs and financial

Plan A __HMO 3000 Deductible__

Aspect/Calculation

Cost Per Pay Period $ __43.84__

Number of Pay Periods __26__
(i.e. 52, 26, 24, or 12)

Multiply the 2 lines together

Total Cost Per Year $ __1,139.84__

Health Plan Maximum Out-of Pocket Costs $ __8,700.00__
(annually)

Plan B __HMO 250 Deductible__

Aspect/Calculation

Cost Per Pay Period $ __90.41__

Number of Pay Periods __26__
(i.e. 52, 26, 24, or 12)

Multiply the 2 lines together

Total Cost Per Year $ __2,350.66__

Health Plan Maximum Out-of Pocket Costs $ __1,500.00__
(annually)

Each of these AvMed options of health offers both peace of mind and financial security. Withhold

---

Plan A _____

Aspect/Calculation	
Cost Per Pay Period	$ _____
Number of Pay Periods (i.e. 52, 26, 24, or 12)	_____
Multiply the 2 lines together	
Total Cost Per Year	$ _____

Health Plan Maximum Out-of Pocket Costs $ _____
(annually)

Plan B _____

Aspect/Calculation	
Cost Per Pay Period	$ _____
Number of Pay Periods (i.e. 52, 26, 24, or 12)	_____
Multiply the 2 lines together	
Total Cost Per Year	$ _____

Health Plan Maximum Out-of Pocket Costs $ _____
(annually)

Plan A _____

Aspect/Calculation

Cost Per Pay Period $ _____

Number of Pay Periods   _____
(i.e. 52, 26, 24, or 12)

Multiply the 2 lines together

Total Cost Per Year $ _____

Health Plan Maximum Out-of Pocket Costs $ _____
(annually)

Plan B _____

Aspect/Calculation

Cost Per Pay Period $ _____

Number of Pay Periods   _____
(i.e. 52, 26, 24, or 12)

Multiply the 2 lines together

Total Cost Per Year $ _____

Health Plan Maximum Out-of Pocket Costs $ _____
(annually)

Use these pages for your calculations.

Other Funding Methods to Pay for Out-of-Pocket Expenses

With rising healthcare costs and increased financial responsibilities, out-of-pocket expenses have become a significant consideration for those who need medical care. Fortunately, there are several funding mechanisms available to assist with these out-of-pocket expenses. Understanding these options can help individuals make informed decisions about how to manage and offset these costs.

- **Gap Plans**: Gap plans serve as a safety net for those who have group health insurance. These plans are designed to help cover the costs that might be left by the primary insurance. Key features include:

  Coverage of Deductibles: One of the primary benefits is the coverage of deductibles, ensuring that the policyholder does not have to pay the entire amount themselves.

  Coverage of Out-of-Pocket Maximums: Some gap plans may even cover the maximum out-of-pocket costs, ensuring further protection against large medical bills.

  Gap plans often have different coverage levels for services for inpatient hospital services and out-patient services. If you are considering a gap plan, make sure to read all the details carefully. If you have more questions, ask your insurance agent, broker, or plan administrator for clarification.

Also, keep in mind that while some gap plans offer coverage for prescription drugs, is not common. So if prescription coverage is important to you, check to see if your gap plan includes it.

- **FSA (Flexible Spending Account) Plans:** Flexible Spending Accounts offer a way for employees to set aside a portion of their earnings to pay for qualified medical expenses. Features of FSA plans include:

  Pre-Tax Deductions: Money set aside in an FSA is deducted from an employee's paycheck before taxes, reducing taxable income.

  Use It or Lose It: A notable characteristic of FSAs is that if the funds are not used by the end of the plan year, they are forfeited. It is crucial for individuals to estimate their medical expenses accurately to avoid losing unused funds.

  You can use your FSA to pay for a wide range of items and services. Here is a simplified list of items and services for which you can typically use your FSA:

  Doctor's Office Copays
  Prescription Medication

Eyeglasses
Contact Lenses
Over-the-Counter Medicines
Dental Work (e.g., fillings, braces)

First Aid Supplies
Pregnancy Test Kits

Please note that it's always a good idea to check your specific FSA guidelines, as eligibility for certain items can vary.

HSA (Health Savings Account) Plans: Health Savings Accounts function like personal savings accounts, but the money can only be used for qualified medical expenses. Here is what you need to know:

- **Tax-Free Deposits:** Contributions made to an HSA are not subject to federal taxes, and can be funded by both the employer and employee.

- **High Deductible Health Plan Requirement:** To be eligible for an HSA, an individual must be enrolled in a High Deductible Health Plan (HDHP).

- **Roll-Over Benefits:** Unlike FSAs, HSAs allow unused funds to roll over to the next year, providing a way for individuals to save for future medical expenses.

You can use your HSA for a wide range of medical expenses. If you have a high-deductible health plan, you can tap into your

HSA to cover costs that your insurance does not fully cover. The scope of what you can use your HSA for is surprisingly extensive. Here is a sample list of eligible expenses:

- Doctor Visits: Both primary care and specialist consultations.

- Hospital Stays: Room charges, surgical procedures, emergency care, and related treatments.

- Prescription Medications: Any medication prescribed by a doctor.

- Over-the-Counter Medications: As of 2020, you can use your HSA for OTC medications without needing a prescription.

- Dental Care: Cleanings, fillings, crowns, and orthodontic treatments.

- Eye Care: Exams, eyeglasses, contact lenses, prescription sunglasses, and LASIK surgery.

- Mental Health Services: Therapy, counseling, and psychiatric services.

- Laboratory Tests: Blood tests, biopsies, MRIs, CAT scans, and other diagnostic services.

- Physical Therapy and Rehabilitation: Post-injury or surgery recovery treatments.

- Chiropractic Care: Spinal adjustments and other chiropractic treatments.

- Medical Equipment: Items like crutches, wheelchairs, and blood pressure monitors.

- Maternity Care: Pre- and post-natal care, including birthing classes and lactation supplies.

- Smoking Cessation Programs: Prescription medications and program fees related to quitting smoking.

- Preventative Services: Vaccines, mammograms, and colonoscopies.

- Hearing Care: Hearing aids, batteries, and hearing exams.

- First Aid Supplies: Bandages, antiseptics, and first aid kits.

- Transportation: Ambulance fees and certain types of travel to and from medical facilities.

- Long-Term Care Insurance: Premiums can sometimes be paid using HSA funds, based on age and other factors.

- Home Improvements for Medical Reasons: Ramps, handrails, and other home improvements for medical necessity can sometimes be included.

It is a good idea to consult the latest IRS guidelines or your plan administrator to confirm that an expense is HSA-eligible. Laws and rules may change, so staying updated will help you make the most of your HSA funds.

And remember, you can use the funds in your HSA only for qualified medical expenses.

HRA (Health Reimbursement Arrangement) Plans: HRAs are employer-funded plans that reimburse employees for out-of-pocket medical expenses. Key features of HRAs include:

- **Employer-Funded:** Only employers can contribute to an HRA; employees cannot.

- **High Deductible Health Plans:** HRAs are often paired with HDHPs, though not exclusively.

    - **Flexible Design:** The employer decides on the design of the HRA, including what expenses are covered and how much can be reimbursed.

Creative Funding Mechanisms

Keep in mind that you might have other funding mechanisms when something unexpected happens. Take for example a car accident. There could be special coverage in your auto insurance to help with costs. So always investigate all your options!

In the aftermath of a car accident, victims are often faced with a flurry of concerns, ranging from physical injuries to the emotional trauma of the event. But one immediate concern is the financial impact of the accident, especially when it comes to medical bills and potential loss of income. Personal Injury Protection (PIP) is an often overlooked yet crucial component.

Personal Injury Protection, more commonly referred to as PIP, acts as a safety net for policyholders. PIP is specifically designed to cover many of expenses that can arise following an auto accident. At its core, PIP primarily covers medical expenses, ensuring that injuries sustained in the accident do not lead to exorbitant out-of-pocket costs for the victim. Moreover, beyond just medical expenses, PIP can also offer coverage for lost wages, providing a buffer against the financial strain of missed workdays.

Insurance companies offer varying degrees of PIP coverage. While some might provide a limit as low as $2,500, others can extend this limit to $5,000, $10,000, or even more. This range in coverage provides policyholders with the flexibility to tailor their PIP coverage based on their individual needs. For instance, individuals with health insurance plans that have high out-of-pocket costs might consider opting for higher PIP limits on their auto policy. This strategy ensures that, in the unfortunate event of an accident, the heightened PIP coverage can help bridge the financial gap left by their health insurance.

However, a word of caution is warranted here. It is crucial to note that PIP coverage is exclusively meant for auto accidents. Thus, while it can be a valuable addition to one's overall insurance portfolio, it should not be mistaken as a replacement for comprehensive health insurance.

In situations where an accident occurs due to the fault of another driver, the landscape changes slightly. In such cases, the at-fault driver becomes financially responsible for the victim's medical expenses, potentially covering the latter's out-of-pocket costs. But what if the at-fault driver is uninsured or underinsured? This is where the provision of uninsured or underinsured motorist coverage comes into play. If included in one's policy, this coverage kicks in to cover expenses when the other party is unable to. It is a layer of protection against the unpredictability of other drivers on the road.

However, the intricacies of auto insurance, and especially PIP, can vary significantly based on state laws and regulations. As such, it is advisable to have a consult with an auto insurance agent or broker. These professionals can offer insights tailored to individual needs and the specific nuances of the state in which one resides.

In conclusion, while the intricacies of medical costs can be overwhelming, a variety of funding methods exist to help you navigate and manage out-of-pocket expenses. By leveraging these mechanisms, you can have peace of mind and focus on what is truly important – your health.

Chapter 6

Ancillary Coverages

In addition to standard health insurance, many employers offer a comprehensive suite of group ancillary coverages designed to protect your well-being. These often-overlooked benefits encompass group dental insurance for oral health, group life insurance for your family's financial security, and group vision insurance to maintain your vision. Additionally, there are group short-term and long-term disability coverages to safeguard income in the event of illness or injury, as well as specialized group cancer plans to assist with the financial burdens associated with cancer treatment. Collectively, these ancillary benefits play a critical role in enhancing the overall compensation package, serving to protect aspects of your life.

Dental Insurance

Dental insurance is the second most requested group insurance benefit. Think of dental insurance as a safety net for your smile. Taking care of your teeth is about more than just maintaining a bright smile. Poor dental health can lead to issues like gum disease, which has been linked to heart disease, diabetes, and even stroke. Regular visits can catch problems early before they become a bigger, more expensive, and painful issue.

The dental insurance market can be quite varied and complex, and plan designs often differ from one insurance provider to another. However, I can give you a general overview of some common types of group dental insurance plan designs commonly found in the market as of my last update in September 2021. Keep in mind that specific plan offerings might vary by provider and region.

Group Dental Plan Types

There are many group dental insurance plans on the market today with many variations. Here are some of the most common:

Dental Health Maintenance Organization (DHMO)

- Pros: Low premiums, no deductibles, no annual limits.

- Cons: Limited network of providers, must choose a primary care dentist.

DHMO plans have network dentists, and it is important to get your dental care within this network to maximize your savings. You will need to choose a primary dentist. If you need specialized care, your dentist will refer you to an in-network specialist. One of the key advantages of a DHMO plan is its affordability. The monthly payments are generally lower, and many routine services such as cleanings and X-rays may be fully covered. However, a limitation is the restricted choice of dentists. You will need to make sure your preferred dentist is in-network to get the most out of your plan. If your dentist is not in the network, you will need to choose a different dentist from the list. If budget-friendly, routine dental care is your priority and you are comfortable choosing from a list of providers, a DHMO could be a good fit for you.

Group Dental Preferred Provider Organization (DPPO)

One standout feature of a DPPO is its flexibility. You can choose to see either "in-network" or "out-of-network" dental providers and many DPPO plans offer the same level of benefits whether you are in-network or an out-of-network. However, there is a significant incentive to staying in-network: you are protected against "surprise" or balance billing.

Should you decide to go out-of-network, be prepared for what is known as "reasonable and customary" charges. These are fees that exceed what your insurance company pays, and you are responsible for the difference.

Another detail to consider is the pre-existing conditions clause. If you opt not to enroll during the initial open enrollment period, you will need to wait for the next open enrollment period or have a qualifying event to enroll. Even then, if you have not had dental coverage in the past 12 months, you may face some restrictions. The pre-existing conditions clause could prevent coverage for major dental services for up to a year, depending on the terms of the contract.

Lastly, if you are new to the plan and have specific dental needs involving endodontics (root canals, for instance) or periodontics (gum treatments), it is crucial to consult with your insurance agent, broker, or plan administrator. Your employer may have opted to include these as "Type 2 services." This means even if you are in a waiting period due to the pre-existing conditions clause, these particular treatments might still be covered.

- Pros: Larger network of dentists, flexibility to see out-of-network providers.

- Cons: Higher premiums, some deductibles ($25 to $50 in most cases), and annual maximums. However some plans can offer unlimited annual maximums depending on the carrier.

Understanding these nuances can help you make an informed decision, ensuring that you select a dental plan that aligns with both your health needs and your financial situation.

Dental Indemnity Plans

Dental Indemnity Plans offer the freedom to choose any dentist you like, but there are a few important details to keep in mind. First, these plans often operate on a "reasonable and customary" charge basis, meaning the insurer will only cover what it deems a standard fee for dental services in your area. If your chosen dentist charges more, you are responsible for the difference. Another crucial point is, like the DPPO, the pre-existing conditions clause generally applies. If you decide not to enroll during the open enrollment period, you will need to wait for either another open enrollment or a qualifying event, like a marriage or job change, to sign up. Moreover, if you have not had dental insurance in the past 12 months, this clause might prevent the plan from covering major services like oral surgery or crowns for the first year, depending on your contract. Because of these intricacies, if you are considering a Dental Indemnity Plan, it is a good idea to consult your agent, broker, or plan administrator to clarify how specific treatments, such as endodontics (root canals) and periodontics (gum treatments), are covered. This makes it crucial to understand the details before making your choice.

- Pros: Complete freedom to choose any dentist, no network restrictions.

- Cons: Highest premiums, deductibles, and copayments; may require paperwork for reimbursement.

Discount Dental Plans

Discounted Dental Plans are often mistaken for insurance, but they operate differently. Instead of paying monthly premiums and getting partial or full coverage for various treatments, a Discounted Dental Plan offers you reduced rates on the dental services from a network of dentists. After paying an annual or monthly membership fee, you are eligible to receive services at reduced rates. This can range from 10% to 60% off standard pricing, depending on the treatment. These plans do not offer any financial reimbursement; they simply provide a discount at the time of service. The appeal of such plans lies in their simplicity and immediate effectiveness—there are usually no waiting periods, deductibles, or complicated claim forms to navigate. However, you must stay within the network of dentists to receive the discounts. Another limitation to consider is these plans might not offer as comprehensive a list of services as traditional insurance plans. Before you opt for a Discounted Dental Plan, make sure to review the list of participating dentists and the range of services offered at discounted rates. Since these are not insurance plans, they can often be used in conjunction with traditional dental insurance to maximize your savings on dental care.

- Pros: Reduced fees for a variety of services, affordable.

- Cons: Not insurance, just a discount; must use in-network providers.

Remember to consult with your HR department, benefit consultant, agent or broker to discuss which plan design best meets your personal needs and circumstances.

Group Vision Insurance

Vision insurance plays a vital role in promoting eye health and well-being among employees. It not only covers routine eye examinations, but also provides for prescription eyeglasses, contact lenses, and sometimes even laser surgeries. Here is a list of the common plan designs:

- Basic Plans - Basic group vision insurance plans generally cover routine eye exams, and they may offer some level of discount on prescription eyewear or even include a small allowance toward purchases. These plans often come with minimal premiums and are a part of a more comprehensive health insurance package.

- Mid-Tier Plans - These plans offer more than just basic coverage. Apart from routine eye exams, they may offer more generous allowances for frames and lenses and may even cover specialty lenses like progressives or photo-chromic lenses. The premiums for these plans are moderate.

- Premium Plans - Premium plans offer the most comprehensive coverage options. These can include higher allowances for designer frames, coverage for specialized treatments such as orthokeratology, and even partial coverage for laser eye surgery. The premiums are comparatively higher but offer the best range of services and product choices.

Waiting Periods for Vision Plans

Most plans offer immediate coverage, particularly for eye examinations and basic prescription eyewear. This means employees can take advantage of the benefits as soon as they are enrolled. Some plans may have graduated waiting periods. For instance, routine eye examinations might be covered immediately, but there might be a 3 to 6-month waiting period for lens and frame allowances. More complex procedures like laser eye surgery might have a waiting period of a year or more.

Network Requirements

Vision plans usually have a network of service providers, including optometrists and ophthalmologists, where employees must go to receive the full benefits of their plan. If your plan offers an out-of-network benefit, this often results in higher out-of-pocket costs. Check you plan carefully to insure you are making the most of your vision plans.

Group vision insurance premiums are relitivly low and is a valuable addition to any employee benefits package. It not only aids in maintaining eye health but also provides financial support for vision correction, thus enhancing the overall well-being and productivity of employees. Understanding the intricacies of various plan designs, waiting periods, and network requirements can help both employers and employees make informed decisions.

Sample Vision Plan

Below is a sample outline of a group vision insurance plan design, detailing the benefits, costs, and other features. Your plan may vary. HINT: Common plan codes are the maximum benefit on the plan. For example, Plan 150 may be the maximum benefit it pays for specific items.

Routine Eye Examinations

- In-Network: 100% covered, limited to one exam per calendar year

- Out-of-Network: Reimbursement up to $45

Prescription Eyeglasses and Frames

- In-Network: $150 allowance, then 20% off any overage; one frame per calendar year

- Out-of-Network: Reimbursement up to $70
  Lenses (per pair)

- In-Network: $25 copay; includes single vision, bifocal, and trifocal lenses

- Out-of-Network: Reimbursement up to $40

Contact Lenses (instead of eyeglasses)

- In-Network: $130 allowance, then 15% off any overage; limited to one purchase per calendar year

- Out-of-Network: Reimbursement up to $100

Laser Eye Surgery

- In-Network: 15% off regular price or 5% off promotional price

- Out-of-Network: Not Covered

Waiting Periods

- Routine Eye Examinations: Immediate coverage

- Prescription Eyewear**: 3-month waiting period

- Laser Eye Surgery**: 12-month waiting period

Remember, this sample vision plan design. It outlines the essential elements that <u>might</u> be included in a real-world vision plan. Check with your Broker, Agent or Plan Administrator for details of your plan.

Group Life and Accidental Death & Dismemberment (AD&D)

Group life insurance is offered to a group of people, typically employees of a company or members of an association. The idea is simple: if you pass away while the policy is active, it provides a payment, known as a death benefit, to your chosen beneficiaries—often your family or loved ones.

Group policies are usually less expensive than individual policies due to the risk being spread across many individuals. Employers often offer group life insurance as part of a benefits package, sometimes covering the cost entirely or sharing it with employees.

Accidental Death & Dismemberment (AD&D) insurance provides additional coverage in the case of accidental death or certain severe injuries. If you were to pass away due to an accident, like a car crash, the policy would provide an additional payment in addition to your group life insurance. It also covers specific injuries, such as loss of limb or eyesight, with a payout that is a percentage of the policy's face value.

AD&D is often offered as a "rider," or add-on, to a group life insurance policy. You can opt for AD&D coverage when you sign up for your group life insurance, or you might even find it automatically included in your benefits package.

Group Life Insurance Portability

One of the significant features of many group life and AD&D policies is "portability." This means you can "take the policy with you" if you leave your job. Portability can be a lifeline for maintaining your coverage while between jobs or transitioning to a new one.

To make your policy is portable, you will generally have a set period—often 30 to 60 days—after leaving your job to convert your group policy into an individual policy. The premiums may be higher once you make this conversion as the group discount no longer applies.

Schedule of AD&D

AD&D policies come with a "schedule," which is essentially a list that outlines the payout for various types of injuries. For example:

- Loss of one limb might be 50% of the policy's face value.

- Loss of eyesight in one eye might be 25%.

- Paralysis could be 75%.

It is essential to read this schedule carefully to understand the extent of your coverage.

Understanding the terms and benefits of group life and AD&D insurance can offer peace of mind and significant financial relief to your loved ones in the case of your unexpected death or severe injury. By understanding the basics, features like portability, and how to read the schedule of AD&D, you can make informed decisions about your coverage options.

Remember, while the terminology might seem complicated at first glance, the purpose behind these insurance policies is simple: to offer financial security in uncertain times. So, take the time to understand your options, and you will be better prepared for whatever comes your way.

Short-Term Disability Insurance

Short-term disability insurance provides financial coverage in the form of a percentage of your salary when you are unable to work due to an illness, injury, or other qualifying condition that is non-work related. Short-term disability helps cover your bills and expenses while you are off work and recovering. Typically, short-term disability pays for a few weeks to a few months, commonly ranging from 13 to 26 weeks, although this can vary depending on your policy.

Why Is Electing Short-Term Disability Insurance is Important

Medical expenses can pile up quickly, and even with the best of health insurance plans, out-of-pocket costs can leave a dent in your savings. Add to that your routine bills like mortgage or rent, utilities, and groceries. Without a regular income, managing these costs becomes a colossal mess. Short-term disability insurance acts as a financial buffer, softening the impact of these expenses.

You might think, "I have paid time off (PTO), so I'm covered, right?" Well, PTO can run out much faster than you anticipate, especially when you are out of work for an extended period of time.

The Costs: Group Short-Term Disability vs. Individual Disability Insurance

One of the most significant benefits of opting for a group short-term disability plan through your employer is the cost-effectiveness. On group plans, the risk is spread out over many people, which generally translates to lower premiums for you.

Another advantage to group disability plans is the simplified underwriting process. Individual disability insurance often requires detailed medical exams and questionnaires. Another feather is the simplified premium payments. In most cases, short-term disability insurance premiums are deducted directly from your paycheck. This automatic process makes it easier for you to manage payments.

REMEMBER: Do not pretax disability premiums. If you do, the benefits are taxed. It is cheaper to pretax the premiums than the benefit.

Elimination Periods

The "elimination period" is essentially a waiting period before your benefits kick in. This period can range from zero days up to two weeks or even longer. During this time, you cannot receive disability payments, so it is crucial to have small savings to cover immediate expenses.

Group short-term disability insurance offers peace of mind for a relatively low cost, especially when compared to individual plans. This safety net can save you from financial hardship when an injury or illness occur.

Long-Term Disability Insurance

Long-Term Disability Insurance provides a portion of your income if you are unable to work due to a disabling condition typically exceeding 90 days. LTD policies generally cover 60-80% of your pre-disability earnings and can last for several years or until retirement age, depending on the policy's terms.

The duration of coverage varies and is usually outlined in the policy. Your employer may have chosen a policy that offers benefits for 2 years, 5 years, or until you reach the age of 65 or even 67 in some cases. Some policies also provide lifetime benefits, although these are rare and expensive.

The Elimination Period

The elimination period for LTD is typically 90 days but can range between 30 to 365 days. This is the waiting period between the onset of your disability and when your LTD benefits begin. You must be disabled continuously through this period to qualify for benefits. If your employer is offering Short-Term

Disability Insurance (STD), it generally coordinates with your LTD plan. Having both LTD and STD can provide comprehensive income protection. Here is how they can work together:

- Initial Phase: If you become disabled, your STD policy kicks in first, usually after a very short elimination period.
  Most STD plans pay benefits weekly whereas LTD benefits pay monthly.

- Intermediate Phase: Once STD benefits are exhausted, and if you are still disabled, LTD takes over after its elimination period.

While STD policies cover immediate, short-term needs, LTD plans are designed for long-term financial stability. Understanding the coverage duration and elimination periods is crucial for maximizing the benefits from both types of disability insurance. Having both in your financial portfolio ensures that you are covered for both short-term occurrences and long-term challenges, providing complete peace of mind.

Cancer Plans

Group cancer plans are specialized policies designed to provide financial assistance specifically for the treatment of cancer. Unlike health insurance, these plans focus solely on the costs related to cancer treatment, including hospitalization, chemotherapy, radiation, surgery, and sometimes even aftercare. These plans are often offered to groups—typically employees of a company or members of an organization—at a discounted rate.

One of the most attractive features of a group plan is the cost. Because the risk is spread over a larger number of people, the premiums are generally lower than those of individual plans. In addition, group cancer plans require minimal or no underwriting. This means that individuals might not have to undergo medical tests to be eligible for the plan, making the enrollment process easier and faster.

Individual vs. Group Cancer Plans

Group plans are generally more affordable but might offer less customization compared to individual plans. Compared to group plans, individual cancer plans may offer more comprehensive coverage options, including the choice of medical professionals and facilities. Group plans may limit these choices to an extent. Also, the individual plans are portable, meaning they stay with you regardless of your employment status. Group plans, on the other hand, are often tied to your job or employment with a company.

Advantages of Group Cancer Plans

- Affordability: Lower premiums due to collective bargaining.

- Ease of Access: Simplified underwriting process.

- Additional Perks: Access to wellness programs and specialized cancer centers.

- Community Support: Being part of a group can offer a sense of community, which is vital during tough times.

Group cancer plans can be a lifeline, providing financial relief and peace of mind during a difficult period. Remember to always read the fine print, consult your agent, broker, financial and medical advisors, and consider your individual circumstances before making a decision.

Chapter 7

Qualifying Events: A Detailed Breakdown

This chapter focuses on qualifying events, also known as 'life changes,' that have a direct impact on your health insurance coverage. It aims to provide insights and practical tips to help you navigate these significant moments effectively.

Your group insurance coverage allows for various qualifying events, which are essentially significant milestones in your life. These events allow you or your dependents to either enroll in, modify, or even terminate your health insurance outside of the typical annual open enrollment window. Keep in mind the specifics may vary based on your employer and insurance provider. Below, is a list of the common qualifying events:

- New Employment

- Probationary Period Completion

- Marriage

- Divorce or Legal Separation

- Birth or Adoption

- Death of a Covered Dependent

- Job Loss

- Retirement

- Reduction in Hours

- Change in Job Role

- Moving Out of Area

- Relocation for Work

- Employer Switches Plans

- Cessation of Employer Contribution

- Turning 26

- Turning 65

- Loss of Other Coverage

- COBRA Expiration

- Military Service

- Government Orders

- Disability

Failure to report these qualifying events to your employer or HR department, typically within 30 days, could result in losing your opportunity to make plan changes until the next open enrollment period.

Qualifying Events: A Detailed Breakdown of Each Event

This section offers recommendations for managing each qualifying event. Remember to do your research, and if you have questions, consult your HR department, plan administrator, agent, or broker.

New Employment

Starting a new position is considered a qualifying event, providing you a window to enroll in, change, or decline group health insurance. Here is a break down what you need to know about handling your health insurance while you enter this new phase.

Before making your choices, ensure you understand the essentials of the group health insurance offered by your new employer. Different companies offer different types of plans, with various coverage options, premiums, and benefits. Get a grasp of the following:

- **Types of Plans:** Whether it's an HMO, PPO, or another type of plan, understand what is available.

- **Costs:** Know the monthly premiums, copays, and deductibles associated with each plan.

- **Coverage:** What types of medical services are covered? Are your current physicians in-network?

- **Waiting Period:** Is there a probationary period before your new health insurance kicks in?

When Enrolling in a Plan

- **Review the Paperwork:** Your HR department will likely provide a benefits package, either digitally or in print.

- **Compare Plans:** Weigh the pros and cons of the available options based on your medical needs and financial situation.

- **Talk to HR:** If you have questions or uncertainties, consult your Human Resources department for clarifications.

- **Fill Out the Forms:** Once you have made your decision, complete the enrollment forms by the deadline provided. Read it carefully and make sure it is complete and legible. The following information is absolutely required for you and your dependents: Name, Date of Birth, Date of Hire, Address, Social Security Numbers.

Coverage During the waiting period

If you have a waiting period with your new employer, you can choose to elect COBRA or State Continuation from your previous employer. If you did not have coverage with your previous employer, may opt for an individual short-term medical plan. These plans have limitations and may require medical underwriting so ask your agent or broker for details.

Important Timelines

Typically, you need to complete your enrollment within 30 days of your start date, though timelines can vary by employer. Failure to do so could result in waiting until the next open enrollment period to obtain coverage.

Take the time to understand your options and choose the best coverage for you and your family. Remember, this is more than a checklist item; it is a significant step in securing your health and wellbeing as you venture into this new phase of your career.

Probationary Period Completion

Probationary periods serve as a sort of "trial run" for new employees, and they often also serve as a waiting period for accessing full benefits, like health insurance coverage. The rules surrounding probationary periods can sometimes be complex, and your classification as a permanent or seasonal worker can impact your eligibility for health insurance benefits.

Completing your probationary period usually opens up the door to various company benefits, one of which is often health insurance. This is an important milestone, not just as an affirmation of your performance, but as a significant change in your employee benefits. Once this period ends, you typically have a limited time—usually 30 to 60 days—to enroll in your employer's group health insurance plan.

Steps to Take After Completing Your Probationary Period

1. **Confirm Eligibility:** The first step is to confirm with your HR department that you are now eligible for health insurance benefits.

2. **Review Plan Options:** Go through the available health insurance plans carefully, considering factors like

premiums, coverage, and network limitations.

3. **Enroll:** Once you've chosen a plan that meets your needs, follow your company's specific enrollment process. This may involve filling out forms or enrolling online.

4. **Document:** Make sure to get confirmation of your enrollment and keep all relevant documentation in a safe place.

Seasonal Workers: A Special Case

In some instances you might be classified as a seasonal worker. This can have different implications for your health insurance eligibility. Seasonal employment status often means either delayed eligibility or limited plan options. It is crucial to clarify your status with your HR department and understand how it affects your benefits.

1. **Clarify Your Status:** If you are unsure, confirm whether you're considered a seasonal worker.

2. **Understand the Limitations:** Be clear on how being a seasonal worker affects your eligibility for health insurance benefits.

3. **Explore Other Options:** If your seasonal status limits your benefits, look into other health insurance options such as short-term health plans.

4. **Stay Updated:** If your employment status changes from seasonal to permanent, you may need to go through another waiting period or you may become immediately eligible for full benefits. Always check with your HR department for the most current information.

Completing your probationary period is more than just a job milestone; it is often the key to unlocking crucial health benefits. The steps you need to take may vary slightly depending on your company and your employment status—be it permanent or seasonal—but the core actions remain the same: confirm, review, enroll, and document. Being proactive during this transitional phase can make all the difference in ensuring you and your dependents are adequately covered.

Marriage

Marriage is a life-changing event that not only affects your personal life but also brings significant changes to various financial aspects, including your group insurance benefits. After getting married, you will want to consider combining or updating your insurance policies to better suit your new marital status. This section will help guide you through what you need to know about modifying your group insurance coverage when you get married, as well as how to go about adding stepchildren to your plan.

Notifying Your Insurance Provider - Time-frame

Most group insurance plans allow a specified window of time, usually 30 to 60 days, during which you can make changes to your insurance policy due to a "qualifying life event" like marriage. Missing this window might mean you have to wait until the next open enrollment period, which could leave you and your spouse, as well as any stepchildren, without suitable coverage.

Required Documentation

You will likely need to provide some form of proof to validate the marriage event, such as a marriage certificate. Check with your human resources department or your insurance provider for a complete list of required documents.

Instructions

1. **Consult HR or Insurance Provider:** Contact your company's human resources department or your insurance provider as soon as possible to inform them of your change in marital status.

2. **Gather Necessary Documentation:** Obtain a copy of your marriage certificate and any other required documentation.

3. **Submit Paperwork:** Submit the necessary forms and documents within the specified timeframe to update your policy.

4. **Review Policy Options**: You might have different plans or additional riders to choose from. Review these options carefully, keeping your and your spouse's needs in mind.

5. **Finalize Changes:** Confirm all changes have been processed and reflected in your policy.

Adding Your Spouse

Adding your spouse to your group insurance plan is usually a straightforward process. You will have options to add them to your existing coverage or switch to a family plan. Consider the following:

1. **Costs:** Determine how much it will cost to add your spouse to your plan versus having separate plans.

2. **Coverage:** Ensure that the services your spouse needs are covered under your plan.

3. **Network:** Check if your spouse's healthcare providers are in-network for your group insurance.

Adding Stepchildren to Your Plan – Now is the time

Adding stepchildren to your plan can be just as important as adding your spouse. Here are the steps to follow.

1. **Check Eligibility:** Ensure that your plan allows for stepchildren to be included and note any age restrictions that might apply.

2. **Gather Documentation:** You may need documents such as birth certificates or custody agreements, especially if the children are not legally adopted.

3. **Review Plans:** Just like with adding a spouse, review the family plans available and consider whether they meet your stepchildren's needs.

4. **Submit Paperwork:** Complete the necessary forms and submit them along with any required documentation. Remember, you will need to have the children's date of birth, social security numbers and addresses if they reside with the custodial parent.

5. **Finalize:** Make sure to confirm that your stepchildren have been successfully added to your insurance coverage.

Marriage is a qualifying event that enables you to make vital changes to your group insurance coverage. Failure to act promptly could leave you waiting until the next open enrollment period. Always consult your human resources department or insurance provider for specific guidelines and procedures. By staying proactive and organized, you can ensure that your new family receives the coverage they need.

Divorce or Legal Separation

Divorce or legal separation is a significant life event that impacts multiple facets of your life, from emotional well-being to financial status. It also has a profound impact on your group insurance coverage, notably if you or your spouse are part of an employer-sponsored insurance plan. Failure to understand the implications could result in undesirable consequences, both legally and financially.

Legal Considerations

Before making any changes to your insurance plan or your spouse's coverage, it is critical to consult with your legal advisor. Canceling your spouse's insurance coverage before the divorce is finalized may not only be seen as an antagonistic move but can also lead to legal repercussions. Judges do not take kindly to such actions, especially if it leaves the dependent spouse without necessary medical coverage. In some cases, this could influence the court's decision on matters like alimony and property division. Before taking any steps, consult with your attorney to understand the legal implications.

After a divorce or legal separation, you typically have a few options:

- **COBRA Continuation:** The Consolidated Omnibus Budget Reconciliation Act (COBRA) allows the separated or divorced spouse to continue under the employer's group health insurance plan for a limited period, generally up to 18 months.

- **Individual Coverage:** The dependent spouse can opt for an individual insurance plan.

- **Employer-Sponsored Plan:** If the dependent spouse is employed and their employer offers a health insurance plan, they can switch to that plan.

- **Stay on the Plan:** Some states and specific insurance policies allow ex-spouses to remain on the insured's employer-sponsored plan under certain conditions. Check your state laws and your insurance policy terms.

How to Make Changes

If you are the policyholder, and it is time to remove your ex-spouse from the policy post-divorce (and after consultation with your legal advisor), here is how to do it:

1. **Contact HR:** Your first step should be to contact your Human Resources department. They will provide you with the necessary paperwork and guide you through the process.

2. **Fill Out Forms:** You will be asked to fill out several forms to initiate the change. Ensure all the details are accurate to prevent delays.

3. **Submit Documentation:** You may also need to submit your divorce decree as evidence to remove your spouse from the plan.

4. **Follow-up:** Once all paperwork is submitted, follow up regularly to make sure the changes have been implemented.

Divorce is challenging, but the more you know about how it affects your group insurance, the more prepared you will be. Your action plan should include legal consultation, a review of your options, and the necessary paperwork to enact any changes.

Do's and Don'ts

- **Do** consult your attorney before making any changes to your group insurance.

- **Don't** remove your spouse without legal advice, as it could jeopardize your position in court.

- **Do** thoroughly review all options for insurance coverage after the divorce.

- **Don't** rush through paperwork; ensure all information is accurate and complete.

By being informed and cautious, you can navigate this complicated time in a way that is fair and equitable for all parties involved. Consult your attorney, weigh your options, complete your paperwork, and ensure you are compliant with both the law and the terms of your insurance policy.

By following these steps, you can transition into this new chapter of your life with as much peace of mind as possible, given the circumstances.

Adding a New Child to an Existing Group Insurance Policy

While the rules for adding a child can differ depending on your jurisdiction and specific insurance agreement, most plans have well-defined procedures and timeframes you must adhere to. Failure to comply with these could lead to a gap in your child's health coverage, so it is crucial to act quickly and diligently.

The birth or adoption of a child is considered a "Qualifying Life Event" (QLE) under most group insurance policies. A QLE triggers a special enrollment period, usually lasting 30 to 60 days from the date of birth or adoption. During this period, you can add your new child to your existing policy without waiting for the annual open enrollment period. In most cases, you may be able make changes to your plan designs and add other dependents.

Instructions: Steps to Take for Adding Your New Child

1. **Notify Your Human Resources Department:** As soon as it's practical—ideally within a few days after the birth or adoption—notify your employer's Human Resources (HR) department about the new addition to your family. They will provide you with the necessary forms and guide you through the process.

2. **Obtain a Social Security Number for Your Child:**
   After the birth or adoption, it's crucial to apply for a
   Social Security number (SSN) for your child. For new-
   borns, this can often be done at the hospital as part
   of the birth registration process. For adopted children,
   you may need to visit the Social Security Administration
   (SSA) office with adoption documents. The SSN is frequently required for adding your child to your insurance
   and is necessary for tax purposes.

3. **Gather Required Documentation:** You will need
   specific documents to verify the birth or adoption. These
   may include a birth certificate, adoption papers, or other
   legal documents that establish your relationship with the
   child.

4. **Complete Enrollment Forms:** Your HR department will
   provide enrollment forms to add your new dependent.
   Complete these forms accurately and in a timely
   manner.

5. **Review Coverage Options:** The addition of a new
   dependent may change the cost-benefit analysis of your
   current plan. Consult your benefits guide or speak with
   an HR representative to better understand your options.

6. **Submit Paperwork:** Submit all completed enrollment
   forms and required documentation to your HR department. Keep copies for your records.

7. **Confirmation:** After your paperwork is processed, you will receive confirmation that your child has been added to your policy. Review this confirmation carefully to ensure all details are accurate.

8. **Pay Any Additional Premiums** Adding a new dependent usually increases your insurance premiums. Adjust your budget accordingly.

9. **Obtain Insurance Cards:** Upon successful addition of your child, you'll receive new insurance cards that include their information. Keep these cards in a safe, easily accessible place.

The birth or adoption of a child necessitates prompt action to ensure their inclusion in your existing group insurance policy. This process involves several steps, from notifying your HR department to obtaining a Social Security number for your child. Each insurance carrier and policy may have its own specific requirements, but this chapter provides a general roadmap. Consult your employee handbook and HR department for the most accurate and personalized guidance and ensure that all required steps are completed within the special enrollment period to guarantee your child's health coverage.

Death of Covered Dependent

During this period of grief and mourning, administrative tasks can seem especially burdensome. However, it is important to act promptly to update insurance records and file necessary claims to ensure that all benefits are duly received, and future premium payments are adjusted. This section will guide you through the steps to remove a deceased dependent from your existing group insurance coverage and file a life insurance claim if applicable.

Removing a Deceased Dependent from Existing Coverage

1. **Notify the Human Resources Department:** Contact your company's Human Resources department as soon as possible to inform them of the death. They can guide you on how to proceed with removing the dependent from your group insurance policy.

2. **Submit Required Documentation:** You will likely need to provide a certified copy of the death certificate and complete specific forms to formally remove the deceased from your coverage. Obtain several certified copies of the death certificate from the Vital Records office or through the funeral director as you'll need them for various institutions and claims.

3. **Review Policy for Time Limits:** Some policies have time limits within which changes must be made. Ensure you are aware of these deadlines and act accordingly.

4. **Confirm Removal and Recalculate Premiums:** Once the process is complete, your HR department should confirm that the dependent has been removed and inform you of any changes to your premiums or coverage.

Filing a Group Life Insurance Claim

1. **Review the Policy:** Before filing a claim, read through the life insurance policy or consult HR to confirm that your deceased dependent is eligible for benefits.

2. **Gather Required Documentation:** The insurance company will require a certified death certificate and possibly other documents, such as proof of relationship. Gather these in advance to speed up the claims process.

3. **Complete Claim Forms:** Your HR department or the insurance company will provide claim forms that need to be filled out. Complete these forms carefully and attach the required documentation.

4. **Submit Claim:** Submit the completed forms and necessary documents to the insurance company via registered mail or as directed by your HR department.

Keep copies of all forms and correspondence.

5. **Follow-up:** Track the status of your claim periodically to make sure it's being processed in a timely manner. Keep all correspondence, and do not hesitate to contact the insurer or HR for updates.

6. **Receiving the Benefits:** Once approved, the insurance company will send a check or make a direct deposit for the benefits. These funds are generally tax-free and can be used at your discretion.

Key Points

- **Obtain Several Copies of the Death Certificate:** This document is essential for removing a dependent from your insurance policy and filing any insurance claims.

- **Act Promptly:** Insurance companies and HR departments have specific time limits for these procedures.

- **Document Everything:** Keep copies of all correspondence, forms, and evidence submitted.

- **Consult HR for Guidance:** The Human Resources department can provide specific instructions tailored to your company's policies.

- **Follow-up:** Always track the status of your claim and any changes to your policy.

The loss of a dependent is an emotionally draining experience, but taking these necessary administrative steps can help ease future complications and financial burdens.

Job Loss and Group Insurance Coverage

Job loss is a challenging event that not only impacts your financial stability but also disrupts your access to health care benefits. Losing employer-sponsored health insurance can add an extra layer of stress during an already stressful time. However, you have options to maintain your health coverage, primarily through COBRA and State Continuation.

COBRA: The Consolidated Omnibus Budget Reconciliation Act

COBRA is a federal law that allows you to continue your employer-sponsored health insurance after you've lost your job. Employers with 20 or more full-time employees are generally required to offer COBRA coverage. To qualify, you must have been enrolled in your employer's health insurance plan when you lost your job, and the job loss must not be due to gross misconduct.

Instructions for COBRA Enrollment

1. **Notification:** You should receive a COBRA notification from your employer within 14 days of your last day.

2. **Enrollment:** You have 60 days from the time you receive the COBRA offer to enroll.

3. **Payment:** You will need to pay all of the premiums, including the share that your employer used to pay, plus a 2% administrative fee.

State Continuation Plans

State continuation plans are an alternative to COBRA and can be particularly useful if your employer had fewer than 20 employees, as such small employers are not required to offer COBRA. State laws vary, but generally, you may be eligible for state continuation for a period ranging from 3 to 12 months.

Instructions for State Continuation Enrollment

1. **Check Eligibility:** Consult your state's insurance department to understand the specific rules and duration for state continuation coverage.

2. **Notification:** Ask your employer for state continuation information if it's not automatically provided.

3. **Enrollment:** Usually, you have a limited window (often 30-60 days) to opt into state continuation.

4. **Payment:** Similar to COBRA, you willl be responsible for the entire premium amount.

Misconception About COBRA Costs

Many people are surprised by the high cost of COBRA coverage, but it is crucial to understand COBRA is not inherently more expensive than your employer-sponsored plan. The shock comes from the fact that you are now responsible for paying the full premium yourself, without the employer's contribution.
Previously, your employer was likely covering a significant portion of your insurance costs—sometimes as much as 50% to 100%—which you may not have realized until experiencing the full cost through COBRA.

Understanding your options for health coverage can make the transition less challenging. Whether you go with COBRA or state continuation depends on various factors, including your past employment, the size of your employer, and your state's laws. Always read the fine print, ask questions, and make a calculated decision based on your health needs and financial situation.

Retirement

Transitioning from an employment-based plan to a retiree or Medicare plan.

If you have been relying on an employer-sponsored group insurance plan, transitioning to a retiree or Medicare plan requires careful planning and understanding. This section aims to guide you through this transition, outlining the steps you need to take to ensure that you are adequately covered. It is advisable to consult with an agent or broker who specializes in Medicare for guidance.

Retirement is considered a "qualifying event" for the purpose of making changes to your health insurance coverage. The event allows you to switch from your existing employer-based plan to either a retiree health plan (if your employer offers one) or a Medicare plan. You generally have a limited window of time—often 30 to 60 days—after your retirement date to make these changes without penalty.

Retiree Health Plans

Some employers offer retiree health plans as a benefit for long-serving employees. These plans can vary widely in terms of what they cover and how much they cost. If your employer provides a retiree health plan, you will typically receive information about your options before your retirement date. You may need to act quickly to enroll, so be sure to read all materials carefully.

Medicare

Medicare is a federal health insurance program for individuals aged 65 and over, as well as certain younger people with disabilities. If you are eligible, you will have the option to enroll in various types of Medicare plans, including Medicare Part A (hospital insurance), Part B (medical insurance), Part C (Medicare Advantage), and Part D (prescription drug coverage).

Steps to Take - Before Retirement

1. **Consult Your HR Department:** Talk to your employer's human resources department about your healthcare options after retirement. Determine whether a retiree health plan is available.

2. **Research Medicare:** Visit the official Medicare website or consult a Medicare guide to understand your options.

3. **Check Deadlines:** Both retiree health plans and Medicare have specific enrollment periods. Note these on your calendar to avoid missing out.

4. **Consult a Financial Planner:** Healthcare can be a significant cost in retirement. Consult a financial planner to ensure that you can afford the plan you choose.

Steps to Take - Post-Retirement

1. **Formally Notify Your Employer:** Officially announce your retirement and ask for all necessary documents related to your health insurance.

2. **Compare Plans:** Evaluate the costs and benefits of sticking with a retiree plan versus switching to Medicare.

3. **Enroll:** Follow the enrollment procedures for the healthcare plan you choose.

4. **Notify Your Current Provider:** If you are leaving an employer-based plan, make sure to notify your current insurance provider about the change in your employment status.

5. **Seek Guidance:** If you are unsure, consult insurance agents or Medicare advisors who can guide you through the process.

Whether you decide to enroll in a retiree health plan through your former employer or opt for Medicare, take the time to understand your options. By following these steps, you can make a seamless transition from an employment-based health insurance plan to a retiree or Medicare plan.

Reduction in Hours

Losing eligibility due to a decrease in working hours

Group insurance plans usually have a minimum number of work hours that you must fulfill to be eligible for benefits. For instance, you may be required to work at least 30 hours a week to qualify for health insurance under your employer's plan. If you experience a reduction in working hours that drops you below this threshold, you will lose your eligibility for group insurance.

Upon losing eligibility, your employer is legally obligated to notify you within a specified period, typically 14 to 30 days, depending on your jurisdiction. Along with the notification, you should receive information about your rights to continue health coverage through COBRA or State Continuation programs.

COBRA (Consolidated Omnibus Budget Reconciliation Act)

COBRA is a federal law that allows you to temporarily continue your employer's group health benefits for a limited period—usually up to 18 months. However, you'll have to pay the full premium, including the portion your employer used to pay, plus a small administrative fee.

How to Elect COBRA

1. **Review COBRA Notice:** Read the COBRA notification carefully and understand the deadlines.

2. **Elect for Coverage:** Fill out the COBRA election form and return it before the deadline.

3. **Payment:** Make the initial premium payment to activate your COBRA benefits.

State Continuation Options

Some states offer state-based health continuation programs that act as alternatives to COBRA. These programs vary widely in terms of eligibility, coverage length, and costs.

How to Elect State Continuation

1. **Check Eligibility:** Verify if your state has a continuation program and if you are eligible.

2. **Application:** Submit any required forms or documentation to your employer or directly to your insurance carrier.

3. **Payment:** Make the premium payments as required to maintain your coverage.

COBRA vs. State Continuation

While COBRA typically provides coverage for up to 18 months, State Continuation programs may offer different coverage lengths. COBRA usually costs more since you pay the entire premium, but state programs may be more affordable. Here is what to do:

1. **Consult HR:** Speak with your HR department as soon as you know your hours will be reduced.

2. **Weigh Options:** Consider the costs and benefits of COBRA and State Continuation.

3. **Timely Decisions:** Make sure you adhere to all deadlines to avoid losing coverage.

4. **Seek Expert Advice:** Consult a healthcare advisor to help navigate your specific circumstances.

A reduction in working hours can be a stressful experience, particularly when it affects your health benefits. But understanding your options like COBRA and State Continuation can help you make informed decisions to protect yourself and your family.

Change in Job Role

Changes within the same organization, affecting eligibility or plan options.

A role change can either expand or limit the types of insurance coverage you are eligible for, potentially affecting not only you but also your dependents. This section aims to guide you through the key considerations and steps to follow if your job role changes within the same organization, impacting your group insurance options.

Types of Changes in Job Role that Affect Group Insurance

1. **Promotion:** Stepping up to a higher position may make you eligible for a premium plan that offers more extensive coverage.

2. **Demotion:** Conversely, moving to a lower position might result in reduced eligibility.

3. **Transfer:** Changing departments might also change the plans you can access, especially if your new department has its own set of group insurance options.

4. Transition to Part-Time: Moving from full-time to part-time status could affect your eligibility for certain plans.

Steps to Take After a Change in Job Role

1. **Confirm the Change with HR:** Once you know that a change in your job role is happening, contact your HR department to get a clear understanding of how this change impacts your insurance options.

2. **Review New Plan Options:** You will usually be given a set of new plan options based on your changed job role. Carefully review these options and compare them to your current plan. Take into consideration factors like:

   - Premiums

   - Coverage limits

   - Out-of-pocket expenses

- In-network and out-of-network options

- Coverage for dependents

3. **Consult Your Dependents:** If you have dependents covered under your plan, make sure to consult with them about the changes, especially if there's a change in the medical network or coverage options.

4. **Update Your Selection:** After reviewing the options and consulting with your dependents, update your plan selection as needed. Make sure to complete any paperwork or on-line forms within the stipulated time period to avoid losing coverage.

5. **Confirm Changes:** Once you have made the selection, confirm with HR that the changes have been processed. Also, check that you and your dependents have received new insurance cards if applicable.

6. **Update Your Financial Plan**: A change in your insurance plan, especially if it affects premiums or out-of-pocket costs, should prompt you to update your budget and financial plan.

Being proactive and knowledgeable can help you navigate this transition smoothly and ensure that you and your dependents continue to have the insurance coverage that best fits your needs. Remember, when it comes to group insurance, what you don't know can indeed hurt you. Therefore, take the time to understand your new options and make informed choices.

Moving Out of Area

Adjusting Your Group Insurance Coverage

Moving to a new location can be a life-changing event, especially when it involves moving out of your current insurance network or into an entirely different network. Understanding how to manage your insurance coverage during such transitions is crucial to ensuring that you and your dependents continue to have access to necessary healthcare services.

What Happens When You Move?

Moving to a different area often means that you may no longer have access to the healthcare providers in your original network. Most group insurance plans, like Health Maintenance Organization (HMO) and Exclusive Provider Organization (EPO) plans, have specific networks of doctors and hospitals that you must use to get the full insurance benefits. If you move to a location where these networks are not available, you may find yourself without coverage or facing higher out-of-pocket costs.

PPO Plans as an Alternative

If you find yourself moving to a location not covered by your current HMO or EPO, enrolling in a Preferred Provider Organization (PPO) plan might be a viable option. PPO plans typically offer more flexibility when it comes to choosing healthcare providers, even those out of network, although at a higher cost.

Steps to Take Before You Move

1. **Inform Your Current Insurance Provider:** As soon as you know you are moving, contact your current insurance provider to inform them of the change. Ask for details about what happens to your coverage when you move and inquire about the options available to you.

2. **Evaluate Your Needs and Options:** Research the healthcare services in your new location and compare them to what is offered in your current insurance plan. Take into consideration your medical history and ongoing treatments, if any.

3. **Check With Your Employer:** Consult with your human resources department to find out if the company offers insurance plans that cover your new location. Employers with multiple locations often have more than one insurance option available.

4. **Making the Switch:** If you need to switch plans, follow the procedures laid out by your current insurance provider or your employer. This may involve filling out new enrollment forms, or even paying a higher premium.

5. **Confirm All Changes:** Once you have switched to a new plan or updated your existing plan, confirm all the changes with your insurance provider. Make sure you receive new insurance cards and familiarize yourself with your new healthcare providers and benefits.

Knowing the steps to take and the options available to you, such as enrolling in a PPO plan, will help make your transition smoother.

Action Checklist:

1. **Contact your current insurance provider:** Notify them about your move and ask for advice on maintaining or adapting your coverage.

2. **Consult your employer:** If your insurance is part of a group plan through your job, your HR department will be a critical resource. You can also consult your employers agent or broker for guidance.

3. **Research and Evaluate:** Look into healthcare providers in your new location and assess which type of insurance plan best fits your needs.

By proactively managing your insurance transition, you can make your move a less stressful and more seamless experience.

Employer Changes Insurance Plans

Among the many qualifying events that can affect your group health insurance, the most common is when your employer switches insurance plans. This change can occur for a variety of reasons, such as cost savings for the company, improved benefits, or a corporate merger.

Understand the Changes

1. **Attend Informational Meetings:** Your employer will likely hold informational sessions to explain the new changes. Attend these sessions to gather as much information as possible. Take notes and prepare questions in advance.

2. **Read All Documentation:** Go through all the documentation provided by your employer and the new insurance provider. Pay particular attention to differences in benefits, coverage options, premiums, and co-pays.

3. **List Your Healthcare Needs:** Before choosing a new plan, make a list of your healthcare needs and those of any dependents covered under your plan. This includes physicians, specialists, medications, and any planned medical procedures.

4. **Compare Networks:** Make sure that your current healthcare providers are in-network with the new plan. Going out-of-network can be substantially more expensive.

5. Assess Your Finances: This includes not just the premium, but also deductibles, co-pays, and out-of-pocket maximums.

6. **Discuss with Family:** Make sure to include your family in the decision-making process, especially if the changes will significantly impact their healthcare.

7. **Opt-In or Opt-Out:** Based on your assessment, decide whether to opt-in to the new plan, choose another plan if multiple options are offered, or opt-out entirely if you have another source of coverage (e.g., a spouse's plan).

8. **Complete the Necessary Paperwork:** Once you have made your choice, complete any required enrollment forms before the deadline. Keep copies for your records.

By following these steps, you will be better prepared to make informed decisions and transition smoothly to your new group insurance plan.

Cessation of Employer Contribution in Group Insurance

One of the most appreciated benefits of full-time employment is access to a group health insurance plan, often with the employer covering a substantial portion of the premium. However, circumstances can arise where your employer may cease to contribute to the cost of this insurance. The cessation of employer contribution can have significant ramifications, affecting not just your pocketbook but also your healthcare choices.

Without employer contributions, the entire financial burden shifts to you. Given that healthcare costs are a significant monthly expenditure, this can severely strain your budget. You may be forced to re-evaluate the current coverage options and possibly switch to a less expensive plan, potentially sacrificing the quality of care or provider access.

What Should You Do?

1. **Assess Your Current Needs:** Review your healthcare requirements and those of any dependents covered by your plan. Determine which services are essential and which ones you can forego.

2. **Communicate with HR:** Check with your HR department to understand why the cessation has occurred, how long it will last, and if there are any alternative options available to you.

3. **Comparison Shop:** If you are responsible for the full premium, it may make sense to shop around for other health insurance options. You might find plans through the Healthcare Marketplace or private providers.

4. **Consider Short-Term Health Insurance:** If the cessation is temporary, short-term health insurance could provide a stopgap.

5. **Spousal/Partner Insurance:** If your spouse or partner has access to a health insurance plan, look into the cost and coverage options available through their employer.

6. **Financial Planning:** Factor in the new costs into your budget and consider consulting a financial advisor for a comprehensive understanding of your financial health.

7. **Plan for the Future:** Once you have navigated the immediate crisis, start planning for similar situations in the future. This may include building an emergency fund or exploring permanent individual health insurance options.

The cessation of employer contributions towards health insurance is a challenging event that requires prompt and thoughtful action. By understanding your options and taking a strategic approach to select a new plan or modify existing coverage, you can navigate this difficult period while safeguarding your healthcare needs.

Dependent Turning 26

When your dependent turns 26, they will typically "age out" of your group insurance plan. This often results in the dependent losing health, dental, and potentially even vision benefits that they were previously entitled to under your coverage.

Important Dates

- **60 days before 26th birthday:** You will usually receive a notice from your insurance carrier reminding you of the upcoming change.

- **26th birthday:** The dependent officially ages out and is generally no longer eligible for coverage under the parent's plan.

- **Special Enrollment Period:** After turning 26, your dependent has a limited period (usually up to 60 days) during which they can enroll in a new health insurance plan without waiting for the next Open Enrollment Period.

What Are the Options?

- **Employer-based Insurance:** If the dependent is employed and their employer offers a health insurance plan, they can switch to their own workplace insurance.

- **Marketplace Plans:** They can buy a health insurance policy from the Health Insurance Marketplace. Premiums and coverages vary, so it's crucial to compare options.

- **Medicaid:** In some states, they may be eligible for Medicaid depending on income and other criteria.

- **Catastrophic Plans:** These high-deductible plans are usually available for people under 30 and can provide a safety net in case of severe accidents or illnesses.

- **Short-term Plans:** These offer coverage for a limited

period (usually less than a year) but are not as comprehensive as other options.

Having a dependent turn 26 is a significant event that requires careful planning and quick action. Knowing your options and timelines can help you navigate this transition smoothly, ensuring that your dependent remains covered with suitable health insurance.

Turning 65 - Medicare Eligibility and Group Insurance

This age marks the point at which you become eligible for Medicare. Your eligibility for Medicare can have an impact on your existing group insurance plan, as well as on the group insurance premiums for your employer. This section will cover what you need to know about this qualifying event and the steps you should take. It is extremely important to consult with a Broker who specializes in Medicare as the laws are complex.

Medicare is divided into different parts:

- **Part A:** Hospital insurance, which covers inpatient stays, skilled nursing, and some home health care.

- **Part B:** Medical insurance, which covers doctor visits, outpatient care, and preventive services.

- **Part C:** Also known as Medicare Advantage, a private health insurance plan that provides your Part A and Part B benefits.

- **Part D:** Prescription drug coverage.

When you turn 65, you are usually automatically enrolled in Medicare Parts A and B if you are already receiving Social Security benefits. If not, you have a seven-month initial enrollment period that starts three months before your 65th birthday, includes the month you turn 65, and ends three months after you turn 65.

Impact on Group Insurance

Once you are eligible for Medicare, you can choose to drop your employer-sponsored group health insurance and switch to Medicare, or you can keep your group plan and use Medicare as secondary insurance. Here are some steps you should take:

1. **Consult with HR or Plan Administrator:** The first thing you should do is speak with your Human Resources department about how turning 65 and becoming eligible for Medicare and how will affect the group insurance.

2. **Compare Benefits:** Review the benefits and coverage offered by your employer's plan versus what Medicare provides.

3. **Cost Comparison:** Look at the cost of premiums, deductibles, and co-payments for both Medicare and your group plan.

4. **Coordination of Benefits:** If you decide to keep both, understand how Medicare will coordinate with your employer's plan. Usually, the group plan will be the primary payer.

Small Business Owners Turning 65

For small business owners, having an older demographic can significantly increase the group's overall insurance rates. Therefore, as an owner turning 65, you might be able to help lower the group's insurance premiums by switching to Medicare. Step to take for small business owners:

1. **Consult with your Insurance Broker:** Review your current group insurance contract and discuss potential rate changes with an expert.

2. **Make the Switch:** If it makes sense, enroll in Medicare during your initial enrollment period and remove yourself from the group plan.

3. **Review and Adjust:** Monitor the impact of your decision on the group's insurance rates and adjust as necessary.

By taking these steps, business owners can make informed decisions that may benefit both themselves and their employees when it comes to healthcare coverage.

Loss of Other Coverage

Loosing other coverage is often due to factors such as a spouse losing a job, divorce, or aging out of a parent's plan. This qualifying event occurs when you or your dependent loses existing health coverage from another source, and it opens up a special enrollment period. This can happen due to:

- Job termination of a spouse or partner

- Reduction in work hours affecting benefits

- Divorce or legal separation

- Death of the spouse or partner who held the insurance

- Aging out of a parent's health plan upon turning 26

If you, your spouse, or dependents lose other health insurance coverage, you generally have a limited time frame to inform your employer and make necessary changes to your group health insurance. Here's what you need to do:

1. **Notification:** Notify your employer's Human Resources department immediately upon learning about the loss of other coverage. This is usually required within 30 days of the loss.

2. **Documentation:** You may be required to provide documentation that confirms the loss of other coverage. This could be a termination notice, divorce decree, or other official documents.

3. **Review Your Options:** Depending on your needs, you might want to add a spouse or dependent to your existing coverage or change to a different plan entirely.

4. **Submit Changes:** Once you have made your decision, submit the required forms to your HR department within the special enrollment period. This special enrollment period generally last 30 days from the date of the qualifying event.

5. **Confirmation and Effective Date:** You should receive confirmation detailing your new coverage and effective date. Review the information carefully and keep a copy for your records.

Experiencing a loss of other coverage can be stressful but understanding that it serves as a qualifying event can offer some relief. The most important step is to act swiftly and stay within the time limits imposed by your employer and insurance company.

If you need personalized advice for your specific situation, consider consulting HR, or your company's benefits consultant.

COBRA Expiration

While COBRA can be a safety net, it is important to understand that it is not a permanent solution. Coverage under COBRA generally lasts 18 months, although it may be extended up to 36 months in some cases. As you approach the end of your COBRA coverage period, it is crucial to prepare for what comes next. Here are some steps to guide you through this transitional period:

- **60-90 Days Before Expiration:** You will generally receive a notice from your COBRA administrator informing you that your COBRA benefits will soon expire.

- **30 Days Before Expiration:** This is the ideal time to actively explore your options for continued coverage.

Look into Other Coverage

- **Marketplace Insurance:** Look into plans available through the Health Insurance Marketplace. During the 60 days before your COBRA expires and the 60 days after it ends, you are eligible for a Special Enrollment Period which allows you to enroll in a new plan.

- **Medicaid:** Depending on your income and state of residence, you may qualify for Medicaid. You can apply at any time of year.

- **New Employer Plan:** If you have found new employment, enroll in your new employer's health insurance plan as soon as you are eligible.

- **Private Insurance:** You can also purchase health insurance directly from an insurance company or through a broker.

- **Short-Term Plans:** If you are in good health and waiting for other coverage to start, you may consider short-term health insurance plans.

- **State Continuation:** Some states offer State Continuation Coverage, which can be an alternative after your COBRA coverage expires.

State Continuation Coverage

State Continuation laws vary by state and are often referred to as "Mini-COBRA" laws. These laws typically apply to employers with fewer than 20 employees but may offer an extension of benefits after federal COBRA coverage ends.

Qualifying for State Continuation

1. **Eligibility:** Check if your state has a continuation law and if you are eligible. Requirements often include exhausting your federal COBRA first.

2. **Duration:** State continuation durations vary but are generally shorter than federal COBRA.

3. **Notification:** You usually need to notify your insurance provider within a specific time after your COBRA coverage ends if you intend to opt for state continuation.

4. **Cost:** Like COBRA, you will usually have to pay the full premium cost plus a small administrative fee.

5. **Enrollment:** Fill out any necessary forms and make your first payment to ensure continuous coverage.

Reaching the end of your COBRA coverage is a significant event that requires timely and informed decisions. Between marketplace plans, new employer benefits, Medicaid, private insurance, and State Continuation options, you have a range of alternatives to explore. It is important to weigh the pros and cons of each to find the best fit for your healthcare needs and financial situation.

Military Service

Whether you are entering or returning from military service, understanding the adjustments you need to make to your group insurance plans is critical for maintaining consistent and adequate coverage for you and your dependents. This section will help guide you through this qualifying life event and provide actionable steps to help you adjust your insurance coverage accordingly.

Entering Military Service - What Happens to Your Group Insurance?

- **Federal Protections:** Under the Uniformed Services Employment and Reemployment Rights Act (USERRA), you may have the option to continue your existing employer-based health insurance coverage for you and your dependents for up to 24 months.

- **Military Benefits:** Once you enter active duty, you may become eligible for military-provided insurance plans such as TRICARE.

- **Life and Disability Insurance:** Check your policy details to see how military service affects these benefits, as some policies may have exclusions for war zones or high-risk activities.

Steps for Entering Military Service

1. **Notify Your HR Department:** Before your departure, inform your Human Resources department about your impending military service to discuss your options.

2. **Review and Compare Plans:** Weigh the benefits and costs of keeping your civilian insurance versus moving to military-provided insurance like TRICARE.

3. **Adjust Coverage:** If you decide to keep your civilian insurance, you may need to fill out forms to continue coverage under USERRA. If opting for military insurance, ensure you complete the required paperwork for enrollment.

4. **Life and Disability Insurance:** Consider purchasing additional policies that specifically cover military service, especially if your current plans do not provide adequate coverage.

Returning from Military Service

1. **Reinstatement:** Under USERRA, you generally have the right to be reinstated in your previous job and benefits, including your group insurance, provided you meet certain conditions.

2. **Coverage Gaps:** Be cautious of any gaps between the termination of your military insurance and the reinstatement of your civilian insurance.

3. **Policy Changes:** Your previous employer's policies might have changed during your absence. Review new options available to you.

4. **Notify Your HR Department:** Upon your return, inform your HR department as soon as possible to discuss the reinstatement of your benefits.

5. **Review Coverage Options:** Policies may have changed, and new options may be more suitable for you. Spend time reviewing these changes.

6. **Fill Out Necessary Forms:** Complete any paperwork needed to reinstate or modify your coverage.

7. **Check for Coverage Gaps:** If there are gaps, you may need short-term insurance options to cover this period.

Understanding your rights under federal laws like USERRA, and coordinating with your employer and military benefits, will guide you through a smooth transition. Remember, when in doubt, consult professionals for personalized advice tailored to your unique situation.

Government / Court Orders

Legal obligations and government orders open a special enrollment period. This section will focus on two main aspects that can influence your group insurance status: government-issued child support orders and changes in legal obligations to have health insurance. Understanding these issues is essential for compliance, risk mitigation, and safeguarding benefits.

Orders for Child Support

Government-issued child support orders are legal obligation for one parent to provide financial support to the other parent for the well-being of a child or children. These orders often stipulate that the parent providing child support also extends healthcare coverage if available through their employer.

If you are subject to a government-issued child support order, you may be required to include your child or children on your group health insurance policy provided by your employer.

Steps to Take for Child Support Orders:

1. **Notify Human Resources:** As soon as you receive a government order for child support that includes health insurance provisions, inform your HR department.

2. **Submit Documentation:** Provide all necessary legal documents as proof.

3. **Update Your Policy:** Make sure to add your child or children to your existing group insurance policy during the appropriate enrollment period.

4. **Regularly Review:** Periodically check the terms of the child support order in case of modifications that affect the insurance provision.

Court orders or other changes in legal status may mandate you to acquire or maintain health insurance. For instance, as part of a divorce settlement, you might be required to continue covering your ex-spouse. Such court orders can necessitate changes to your group insurance beneficiaries or even force you to enroll if you have not done so.

Steps to Take

1. **Review the Court Order:** Understand all stipulations relating to health insurance obligations.

2. **Consult with Legal Counsel:** To interpret complex legalese, you might require professional legal advice.

3. **Notify HR:** Inform your HR department about the change in your legal obligations and provide necessary documentation.

4. **Adjust Your Plan:** Make changes to beneficiaries or coverage tiers as needed.

5. **Financial Implications:** Assess how these changes will affect your paycheck and plan accordingly.

6. **Follow Up:** Always review and confirm that changes have been successfully made in the group insurance policy.

Legal obligations and government orders can dramatically impact your group insurance coverage. Failure to comply could result in legal penalties and loss of crucial financial safeguards. Early engagement with your Human Resources department, a thorough understanding of the legal documents, and prompt action are critical for navigating these challenges effectively.

Consult with professionals, both legal and financial, to

assess how these changes affect your broader financial landscape. Remember when it comes to legal obligations and your insurance coverage, ignorance is not bliss—it is risky.

Disability: Becoming disabled

This section intends to provide a you with a comprehensive guide on how to navigate your group insurance coverage options when you become disabled. It covers what types of changes in coverage you may require and provides information on how to apply for Short-Term and Long-Term Disability benefits, if available. Disabilities often increases your healthcare needs and costs. Reassessing your current group health insurance to ensure your plan adequately covers these new expenses.

Short-Term Disability Insurance

Short-Term Disability Insurance provides a portion of your salary for a limited period, often 3-6 months, when you are unable to work due to a disability. This coverage can bridge the gap until you are able to return to work or transition to Long-Term Disability benefits.

Long-Term Disability Insurance

Long-Term Disability Insurance kicks in when your Short-Term Disability benefits run out and provides a portion of your income for an extended period, and in some cases, until retirement age. These policies generally have an elimination period of 30 to 90 days. If you have a long-term disability policy, review the details and file claims as needed.

Life Insurance

Your life insurance needs may also change with a disability, especially if you are the primary earner for your family. You may need to adjust your life insurance coverage to ensure it meets your family's needs. In addition, if you have an accidental death and dismemberment rider on your life insurance policy, you may be able to file a dismemberment claim depending on the nature of your disability.

What Should You Do

1. **Assess Your New Needs:** Discuss your new healthcare and financial needs with your healthcare providers and your family. Estimate your ongoing medical costs and how long you might be unable to work.

2. **Consult Your HR Department:** Contact your HR

department to find out what changes you can make to your existing group insurance coverage and how to apply for Short-Term and Long-Term Disability benefits if available.

3. **Review Plan Options and Apply for Disability Benefits:** Check the coverage details, limits, and exclusions for both Short-Term and Long-Term Disability insurance.

4. **How to Apply for Short-Term Disability (if Applicable):**

   • Submit a formal application, usually available from HR or your insurance provider.

   • Include medical documentation proving your disability.

   • Wait for approval and clarify the terms (like the payout amount and duration).

5. **How to Apply for Long-Term Disability:**

   • Usually, you can transition from Short-Term to Long-Term Disability, but a separate application is often required.

   • Submit updated medical records.

- Wait for approval, understanding that the process can be lengthy and may require additional medical examinations.

6. **Make Necessary Changes to Other Insurance:** If your group insurance includes an annual open enrollment, review your options during this period. Some plans may allow you to change your coverage due to a "qualifying life event" like a disability.

7. **Document Everything:** Keep copies of all forms, medical records, and communications. These documents may be necessary for appeals if your disability claim is denied or for future adjustments to your coverage.

8. **Seek Professional Advice:** Consult a financial advisor or an insurance expert to ensure you're making the most of your available options.

Understanding how to adjust your group insurance and apply for disability benefits can provide crucial financial support during a challenging period. Always refer to your specific plan documentation and consult with professionals for personalized advice.

Chapter 8

Terminating Coverage

When and Under What Circumstances Can an Employee Cancel Coverage

Understanding the terms and conditions under which an employee can cancel their coverage is essential for both employers and employees. Health, dental, or other types of insurance benefits offered by an employer usually come with a set of stipulations outlining the circumstances under which such cancellations can occur. In this chapter we will examine the circumstances imposed by Section 125 of the Internal Revenue Code, and special situations when you can cancel coverage.

Open Enrollment Period

Typically, the most straightforward time for an employee to cancel or change their coverage is during the annual Open Enrollment period. During this time, employees can freely add, drop, or change their coverage options without needing to provide a specific reason.

Qualifying Life Events

Outside the Open Enrollment period, you can usually cancel coverage only if you experience a "Qualifying Life Event" (QLE). The most common QLEs include:

- Marriage or divorce

- Birth or adoption of a child

- Loss of other health coverage

- Moving to a new residence

- Change in employment status (e.g., from full-time to part-time)

- For a more comprehensive list of QLE's see chapter 7.

When a QLE occurs, you generally have a limited time period to make changes (usually 30 to 60 days). Documentation proving the QLE is usually required.

Section 125 and Its Implications

Section 125 of the Internal Revenue Code, also known as a Cafeteria Plan, allows employees to contribute a certain portion of their gross income to a designated account before taxes. These funds can then be used for qualifying expenses like health insurance premiums. Under a Section 125 plan, the IRS imposes certain restrictions on when and how you can cancel or change your elections.

Limitations

- **Irrevocably:** Once you make your elections under a Section 125 plan, you generally cannot change them until the next Open Enrollment period or unless you experience a QLE.

- **Consistency Rule:** Any change in elections must be consistent with the event triggering the change. For instance, if you get divorced, you cannot suddenly decide to add dental coverage; however, you could remove your ex-spouse from your coverage.

- **Timing:** If you do experience a QLE, you have to make the change within the time frame specified by your employer, which is usually consistent with federal guidelines.

- Documentation: You will generally need to provide proof of the QLE within a specified time frame.

If you are enrolled in a Section 125 Cafeteria Plan, your options to cancel or change your coverage are significantly restricted. Therefore, it is essential to be mindful of these limitations when enrolling in or considering changes to your benefits.

Canceling coverage is a decision that comes with both personal and legal considerations. Employees must be mindful of the timing and reason for cancellation, particularly if they participate in a Section 125 Cafeteria Plan, which has stringent federal regulations. Always consult with your Human Resources department or benefits administrator to understand the full scope of your options and limitations.

Chapter 9

Handling Health Insurance Claims

Why Health Insurance Claims Problems Happen

Healthcare is complex even in a perfect world. When we add claims to the mix, the complexity can often be overwhelming. One challenging issue is having a third party, namely the insurance company, paying for medical procedures and services, even though they were not directly involved in the medical consultation or decision-making process.

In most business-related transactions, the payer and the service recipient are the same entity. You pay for a meal, and you eat it. You pay for a book, and you read it. But healthcare often does not work that way, especially when insurance is involved. In healthcare, the patient receives treatment, and the insurance company handles the payment. This disconnect can create a multitude of issues. One of the most common communication gaps is between healthcare providers and insurance companies.

A prime example of such a communication issue arises with the incorrect usage or omission of Current Procedural Terminology or "CPT" codes. CPT codes are essentially the language healthcare providers and insurers use to communicate the services rendered. Every medical, surgical, and diagnostic procedure has an associated CPT code. These codes are crucial for insurance companies to determine how much to pay for a particular service. If a CPT code is missing or incorrect on an insurance claim, the claim is likely to be denied, delayed, or inaccurately processed.

Reasons for Claim Problems

1. **Human Error:** Mis-keying information, submitting claims to the wrong department, or even simple clerical errors can lead to problems in claims processing.

2. **Changes in Pharmacy Benefits Managers (PBM):** PBMs act as intermediaries between insurers and pharmacies. They negotiate drug prices and manage drug benefits for insurance plans. If your company switches PBMs, which happens frequently, coverage for certain medications can change overnight, leading to unexpected costs and denied claims.

3. **Patient Eligibility Issues:** Patients can be ineligible for coverage for a variety of reasons, including lapses in payment, not meeting certain criteria, or even due to clerical errors in the eligibility database.

4. **Changes in Covered Procedures:** Insurance plans frequently update the list of covered and non-covered procedures. If a healthcare provider is not aware of a recent change, they may perform a service that is no longer covered, resulting in a denied claim.

5. **Complex Preauthorization Requirements:** Some insurance plans require preauthorization for certain procedures and medications, adding another layer of complexity to the claims process.

6. **Policy Limitations:** Every insurance policy has limitations and caps, beyond which they will not cover services. Breaching these can lead to partially covered or outright denied claims.

7. **Timing Delays:** Claims often need to be submitted within a certain time-frame to be eligible for payment. Delays in paperwork, either on the part of the healthcare provider or the patient, can lead to denied claims.

Miscommunication and changes in various parameters like PBMs and CPT codes make this a challenging endeavor for all involved parties. Being informed about the intricacies can not only save you money but also protect you from unnecessary stress. Knowledge and communication are your best allies in this complicated but crucial part of modern healthcare. By understanding these challenges and complexities, you can better navigate the world of health insurance claims, ensuring you get the healthcare you need without the financial surprises you don't.

Handling Claims Problems – After the Fact

Health insurance claims can add to an already stressful situation. Whether you have been hospitalized, had surgery, or even just visited your general physician, the last thing you want to face is an issue with your insurance claim. Often, these issues are a matter of coding errors or administrative mistakes rather than an outright denial of your claim.

These steps will guide you through the process and can save you both time and energy:

1. **Do Not Panic:** Upon receiving a rejected claim or an unexpected bill, it is easy to start panicking. However, it is essential to understand that errors are common. The healthcare billing system is filled with codes—each disease, procedure, and even the rooms have their

specific codes. A mere coding mistake could be the cause of your problem. These codes coordinate with each other, and if the codes are a mismatch, the insurance company's computer system can automatically deny your claim.

2. **Call the Number on Your Health Insurance Card for Directions:** Your first step should be to call your health insurance provider for clarity. They can offer instant guidance on why the claim might have been denied or delayed. Make sure to keep a record of these interactions. Note the date, the person you spoke with, and summarize the conversation.

- **Ask for Details:** Limiting your inquiry only to why your claim was denied, dive deeper. Question whether the issue could be related to medical coding, whether all the required documents were submitted, or if additional information is needed from your end. Being specific in your questioning can expedite the resolution process.

- **Verify the Billing Codes:** These billing codes are combinations of letters and numbers that categorize every aspect of your medical treatment, from diagnosis to the procedures performed. Misalignment or errors in these codes are frequent reasons behind claim rejections. Ensure to double-check the codes that were applied to your treatment and query whether they accurately represent what you underwent.

3. **Email or Fax the Bill to the Insurance Company:** After your call, you may be required to email or fax the bill and additional documentation for a formal review. Before sending anything, carefully review all documents for any errors or discrepancies.

   - **Check for Errors:** Go through the document to check if there are any inaccuracies like incorrect codes or misspelled names that could have caused the claim issue.

   - **Include Additional Documents:** Attach supporting documents such as medical records, test results, etc. These can help expedite your claim resolution.

4. **Wait for a Response:** Now comes the hard part, waiting. Your insurance provider could take a couple of days to several weeks to resolve your claim.

5. **Track the Claim:** Most insurance companies offer an on-line service to track the status of your claim. Utilize this to keep yourself updated.

6. **Follow Up if Necessary:** If you do not hear back within the given time frame or the resolution is unsatisfactory, do not hesitate to follow up. A simple phone call or email reminder can often move things along.

When All Else Fails: Contact Your Company's Insurance Broker

If your attempts at resolution through the insurance company prove unsuccessful, your next step should be to contact your company's insurance broker. Brokers usually have experienced support teams who understand the nuances of dealing with insurance company's and medical providers.

- **Leverage Their Expertise:** Your company's broker has an understanding of the complexities involved in insurance agreements and can act as a valuable advocate for you.

- **Provide Full Context:** Give your broker a full history of your claim issue, including the details of all interactions and document submissions.

By following this structured approach, will have the best chance at resolving most insurance claim troubles. Remember, solving a health insurance claim problem is usually a marathon, not a sprint.

Chapter 10

Avoid Non-Network Claims

In the event you have opted for a plan which includes non-network benefits, such as a Preferred Provider Organization (PPO), it is crucial to be careful to avoid non-network claims.

He is an example: If your insurance plan is a PPO and you go to a hospital that is in-network, not all services provided within that facility may not automatically be covered as in-network services. For instance, while you may have an in-network surgeon scheduled for your operation, other providers involved in the procedure—like radiologists, anesthesiologists, and pathologists—may not be in-network.

The Risks of Non-Network Services

Non-network claims can result in significantly higher out-of-pocket costs for several reasons:

- **Separate Out-of-Network Deductible:** You will usually have to meet a separate deductible for non-network services, which is often higher than the in-network deductible.

- **Lower Coinsurance Percentage:** Once your deductible is met, you will often find that the coinsurance (<u>your</u> share of the remaining bill) is higher for non-network services.

- **Higher Maximum Out-of-Pocket Costs:** There is generally a separate—and higher—maximum out-of-pocket cost for non-network services.

- **Usual, Reasonable, and Customary Charges:** Non-network providers may charge what is known as "usual, reasonable, and customary" fees, which are over and above what your insurance policy covers.

Before Surgery or Any Major Procedure

1. **Get a List of Providers:** Ask your surgeon or hospital for a list of all providers involved in your procedure. This should include surgeons, assistants, anesthesiologists, radiologists, and pathologists.

2. **Check the Network:** When you have this list, check with your insurance company to confirm that each provider is in-network.

3. **Get it in Writing:** If possible, get a written confirmation from your insurance company that these providers are in-network.

4. **Pre-Certification:** Another vital aspect of avoiding non-network claims involves pre-certification. Most insurance companies require this formal approval before you undergo any major medical procedure, including surgeries, MRIs, and some treatments. Here is how to pre-certify:

5. **Contact Your Insurance Company:** As soon as your physician recommends a surgery or major procedure, contact your insurance company to start the pre-certification process.

6. **Submission of Medical Documents:** If necessary, your healthcare provider will need to submit documentation that outlines why the procedure is necessary. This can include diagnostic test results, medical history, and treatment plans.

During the pre-certification process, many insurance companies will assign a patient advocate to your case. This advocate can be an invaluable resource for several reasons such as:

- **Guidance:** They can guide you through the complicated landscape of insurance claims, helping you understand what's covered and what is not.

- **Coordination:** They can help coordinate between different departments and ensure that all paperwork is processed in a timely manner.

- **Clarification:** Your patient advocate can answer any questions you have, helping you to understand medical jargon and insurance terminology.

Leveraging the help of a patient advocate is yet another proactive step you can take to avoid unnecessary financial burdens associated with non-network claims.

7. **Read Admission Documentation Carefully:** When you are admitted to a hospital, you are often presented with a mountain of paperwork to sign. Read these documents carefully before signing, as there may be

clauses that make you responsible for additional costs, including fees for non-network providers.

If you find yourself in a situation where you must use a non-network provider, it is often possible to negotiate fees beforehand. Some hospitals and providers are willing to offer a discounted rate if you agree to pay upfront or within a specific time-frame.

Keep meticulous records of all correspondence, bills, and confirmations. These documents can be vital if you have a dispute down the road.

It is easy to assume that since you are using an in-network hospital, all services provided there will also be in-network. This is a dangerous assumption that can cost you dearly. Be proactive, read the fine print, and confirm all details to avoid falling into the trap of non-network claims.

Chapter 11

Handling Insurance Issues at the Time of Service

Navigating the healthcare system can be challenging, particularly when insurance issues crop up unexpectedly. You might find yourself at the doctor's office or the pharmacy, ready to receive the services you need, only to be told that there is a problem with your insurance. If not managed properly, these issues can lead to delays in treatment, and unnecessary stress. This chapter serves as a guide to help you handle insurance issues the moment they arise.

Don't Take Their Word for It

First and foremost, if you are told that there is an issue with your insurance—whether it is deemed inadequate or invalid— do not immediately accept this as the final word. Errors can occur for multiple reasons, such as outdated information in the system, or a staff member might have entered data incorrectly.

Step Away and Call Your Insurance Company

Steps to take to clarify the situation:

1. **Step away from the counter:** Politely excuse yourself and find a quiet spot where you can make a phone call without holding up the line or distracting the service personnel.

2. **Call your insurance company:** Most insurance cards have a customer service number listed on the back. Call this number and speak to a representative about the issue. Make sure to have any relevant information on hand, such as your policy number, to expedite the process.

3. **Be Specific:** Clearly describe the situation, mentioning the type of service you are trying to obtain and what you were told by the service provider.

Hand the Phone Over

After you have spoken to the insurance representative and gained some clarity:

1. **Return to the counter:** Go back to the service counter and explain that you have been speaking to your insurance company.

2. **Hand the phone over:** If the issue remains unresolved or if there are specific points that need clarification, it can be extremely beneficial to have the insurance representative speak directly with the billing staff or the pharmacy team. This direct communication often clears up misunderstandings more efficiently than conveying messages back and forth.

Confirm and Document

After the issue is resolved:

1. **Get confirmation:** Whether the issue was a mistake on the provider's end or an outdated policy at the insurance company, get a confirmation that the problem has been fixed. This can be verbal, but it is advisable to get it in writing via email or a printed statement if possible.

2. **Document the conversation:** Make a note of who you spoke with, the time and date, and the outcome of the conversation for your records. This can be valuable if similar issues arise in the future.

Preventive Measures

- **Regularly Update Information:** Make sure all your details are up-to-date with both your healthcare provider and insurance company.

- **Know Your Policy:** Understanding the specifics of your insurance policy can help you avoid surprises. Make sure you know which services are covered and what your responsibilities are in terms of co-payments and deductibles.

- **Check Before You Go:** Before setting out for the pharmacy or a doctor's appointment, it can be helpful to call ahead and confirm that your insurance is accepted and that all systems are up-to-date.

Insurance issues can be stressful, especially when they interrupt necessary medical services. However, being proactive, knowledgeable, and calm can go a long way in resolving these issues quickly. Remember that the customer service team of your insurance company is there to assist you; do not hesitate to bring them into direct contact with your healthcare provider when needed. By taking these steps, you are not only solving the immediate problem but also contributing to a smoother healthcare experience in the future.

Chapter 12

How Much is Your Doctor Worth

When we ask, "How much is your doctor worth?" We are asking if it is worth paying for a higher priced health insurance plan just to have your preferred doctor in your network.

In the world of health insurance, choosing a health plan with a network that includes your doctor can pose a significant challenge. Occasionally, you may find yourself trying to decide between two diverse health plans that offer distinct networks. This is a common scenario.

Imagine finding yourself at a crossroads where your doctor is in the PPO network but not in the HMO. It is important to calculate the annual costs associated with both plans. Start by determining your annual cost for each option. Then, weigh this against how often you anticipate visiting the doctor over the course of the year. In a situation where you see your doctor infrequently, perhaps once or twice a year, opting for the less expensive option could be more beneficial. Here is a real example to get a better understanding:

Cost of the HMO Plan

- Monthly Premium: $112

- Annual Premium: $1,344

Cost of the PPO Plan

- Monthly Premium: $226

- Annual Premium: $2,712

In this example there are a substantial annual savings of $1,368 if you choose the HMO plan.

Now consider the plans' design components. In this scenario, both have identical deductibles, co-payments, and maximum out-of-pocket costs, but they differ in other significant aspects. The main attraction to the PPO is its larger network and no gatekeeper requirements. While the PPO offers more freedom and a larger network, it comes at a premium price. Unlike the HMO plan, with a restricted network and mandatory gatekeeper requirements, stands as a more budget-friendly alternative.

When faced with these decisions, it comes down to a balance of cost and convenience. Here are some questions to consider:

- How often do you visit your doctor?

- Are the financial savings from choosing the HMO plan substantial enough to warrant changing your doctor?

- Does the broader network and lack of gatekeeper requirements in the PPO plan justify the higher premium?

Making the right choice for you and your family in this situation, simply compare the yearly costs with what you need and prefer in your health plan. In some cases, paying a higher premium may offer peace of mind and greater flexibility, making it worth the extra cost. On the other hand, if your doctor visits are infrequent, the cheaper HMO plan might be your go-to option.

Consider paying your doctor directly.

Paying your doctor in cash can be a practical way to save money. If your preferred doctor is not part of your insurance network, you might notice your premiums are lower; you can set aside the amount you save to use for cash payments during your visits. Depending on your individual circumstances, you might be saving between $1,000 and $2,000 or more every year, especially if you only need to see your doctor once or twice in that time-frame. Additionally, many doctors offer discounts for payments made in cash, so it is a good idea to ask your doctor if this option is available. By opting for cash payments, you can continue seeing the doctor you prefer without the burden of larger premiums charged by your insurance company.

Take a moment to figure out the difference between the more expensive choice and how much you use it. Keep in mind, as the years go by, you might end up using it more, so think through all your options with caution.

Chapter 13

Paying for Health Insurance Out-of Pocket Cost

Healthcare expenses can quickly and being prepared can be a lifesaver. Understanding your options and having a strategy for paying out-of-pocket costs is essential. Out-of-pocket costs refer to the financial obligation that falls on you, including deductibles, co-payments, and coinsurance. This chapter covers the complex world of financing healthcare and offers insights into easing financial stress while ensuring the best possible healthcare.

Understanding Out-of-Pocket Costs

Having a clear understanding of health insurance terms such as "deductibles," "co-payments," and "coinsurance" and "out of pocket maximum" can help you decipher your medical bills and find mistakes. This section will explain these four terms in a simple way.

- **Deductible** - A deductible is the amount you must pay for healthcare services before your insurance begins to pay.

  How Deductibles Work - Suppose your plan's deductible is $1,000. That means for most services, you will pay 100% of your medical bills until the amount you pay reaches $1,000. After that, you share the cost with your insurance company in the form of co-payments, coinsurance, or both.

- **Co-payments** - A co-payment, often referred to simply as "copay", is a fixed amount you pay for a covered healthcare service, typically when you get the service.

  How Co-payments Work - Let's say your primary care doctor's visit has a copay of $20. Each time you visit your primary doctor, you will pay that fixed amount, regardless of the total bill for the visit. If the entire cost of the visit is $150, and your copay is $20, your insurance covers the remaining $130. In some cases, if the billed charges fall under a "procedure" or a "surgical procedure" you may have to pay the co-payment and your deductible.

- **Coinsurance** - Coinsurance is your share of the costs of a covered healthcare service calculated as a percentage (for instance, 20%) of the allowed amount for the service.
How Coinsurance Works - Imagine you have already met your deductible. Now, for subsequent services, you will pay coinsurance. If your coinsurance rate is 20% for a given service and the allowed cost for the service is $100, you would pay $20, while the insurance company would pay the remaining $80.

  Consider this scenario:

  Your insurance has a deductible of $1,000.
  You have a 20% coinsurance.
  Your hospital visit costs $1500.

  If you have not met any of your deductible, you will pay $1000 for the visit, meeting your deductible. Next you will pay your 20% coinsurance on the remaining balance (in this case, 20% of $500 = $100).

- **Out-of-Pocket Maximums** - An out-of-pocket maximum is a cap, or limit, on the amount of money you have to pay for covered services in a plan year. After you reach this limit, your health insurance will pay 100% of the costs for covered healthcare services.

How Out-of-Pocket Maximums Work - Suppose your out-of-pocket maximum is $6,000. This means over the course of your calendar year, once your cumulative deductibles, co-payments, and coinsurance payments reach $6,000, the insurance company will then cover any additional costs for services covered by your plan.

It is important to note that not all of the money you spend on healthcare counts towards this maximum. Premiums, the monthly fee you pay to have health insurance, are not included. Additionally, any services rendered by out-of-network providers, or services not covered by your plan, may not count towards this limit.

Factors Influencing Out-of-Pocket Maximums

Different plans have different out-of-pocket maximums. Some plans might have a lower out-of-pocket maximum, offering you more protection but potentially charging higher premiums as a result. On the other hand, plans with higher out-of-pocket maximums might have lower monthly premiums.

Understanding out-of-pocket maximums is a crucial aspect of managing your healthcare expenses proficiently. It not only assists in selecting the appropriate health insurance plan but also safeguards you from potential financial hardships arising from medical services. Remember to consider the out-of-pocket maximums alongside other elements like deductibles, co-payments, and coinsurance when choosing your healthcare plan to ensure that you are fully covered in any scenario.

Paying for out of pocket expenses

- **Health Savings Accounts (HSAs)**
  Many employers provide Health Savings Accounts (HSAs) as a benefit to their employees. These accounts allow individuals to utilize pre-tax dollars to cover healthcare expenses. If you are enrolled in a High Deductible Health Plan (HDHP), you are eligible to contribute to an HSA with tax-free dollars. Furthermore, if your employer offers to match your contributions, it is wise to maximize this benefit.

  Not only can HSAs be carried into retirement, but accumulating funds in an HSA can also serve as a financial cushion, particularly when you need to meet your deductible or face unforeseen medical expenses. With benefits ranging from tax savings to potential investment growth, HSAs are a powerful instrument for navigating healthcare costs.

- **Flexible Spending Accounts (FSAs)**

  Many companies offer their workers the option to participate in Flexible Spending Accounts, also known as an FSA. It is important to remember that this is a "use it or lose it" deal. Which means that if you do not use the money in your FSA by the end of the year, you will lose it.

  Here is how it works: Say you anticipate you will have $2,000 in medical costs this year. You can put $2,000 into your FSA to cover these costs. This money is taken out of your paycheck before taxes are taken out, spread out over the year.

  Using an FSA is a clever way to save money if you know you will have certain medical costs, such as meeting your deductible or reaching your out-of-pocket maximum, since it is tax-free. So, if you are planning to have medical expenses, make sure to take advantage of your FSA.

- **Gap Plans**

  Gap plans are designed to cover extra costs, including deductibles and maximum out-of-pocket expenses that your group health insurance does not cover. It is a great solution if your employer offers it, giving you a financial cushion in times of need.

These plans specifically help you with the initial expenses, like deductibles — the amount you pay before your insurance kicks in, and maximum out-of-pocket costs — the most you have to pay in a year for covered services. Remember, when you reach your maximum out of pocket on your group health insurance plan it covers 100% of the covered services for the remainder of the calendar year.

In most cases, your company will automatically enroll you in a gap plan, meaning it is not voluntary. However, in some cases, it is voluntary, giving you the choice to opt in or out. Enrolling ins a gap plan can bring peace of mind, knowing you have that extra buffer for your healthcare expenses. It is an extra layer of protection for your wallet, helping you manage those high upfront costs more comfortably.

- **Car Accidents - Covering Out-of-Pocket Costs**
  Car accidents are stressful, and understanding how your car and health insurance can help might bring some peace of mind. It's often possible to use your car insurance to help with health insurance costs, depending on who is at fault.

If the Other Driver is at Fault

If the other person caused the accident and they have car insurance, their bodily injury liability coverage can assist with your health plan's out-of-pocket costs. Keep in mind that settling this might take some time, so keep your healthcare providers informed.

In case where the other driver does not have sufficient insurance or any at all, your own insurance policy might have a safety net. If you have uninsured/under-insured motorist coverage on your auto policy, it can help cover your out-of-pocket expenses, giving you an added layer of protection. This means you can have your medical expenses covered when it comes to car accidents.

If You Are at Fault

When you are at fault, your own car insurance might come to the rescue. There are two key coverages can be inexpensive. Here is what to check for:

Medical Coverage: This part of your car insurance covers only medical bills, helping to meet your health plan's deductible and other out-of-pocket costs right from the start (this is known as "first dollar coverage").

Personal Injury Protection (PIP): This is a more comprehensive option. Aside from medical costs, it might cover lost wages if you are unable to work after the accident.

Being proactive and understanding the overlap of your policies can be extremely beneficial. When you are selecting a car insurance policy, always ensure it blends well with your health insurance, especially in terms of covering out-of-pocket expenses. Being well-informed and making the right choices now can lead to significant savings and fewer headaches should the unexpected occur.

Chapter 14

Preparing for Upcoming Medical Procedures

In the days leading up to a known upcoming medical procedure, are a number of logistics, emotions, and preparations arise. It is a period characterized by anticipation, planning, and ensuring every dollar is effectively used to satisfy the various financial commitments that accompany such procedures. Ensuring a smooth preparation process involves a detailed approach to handle insurance policy verifications, checking HSA or FSA balances, and establishing a rapport with a patient advocate, among other steps. This chapter provides a step-by-step guide to help you with this critical process.

Steps in Preparing for Known Upcoming Medical Procedures

1. **Verify Your Insurance Policy Status**
    Make sure your insurance policy is currently active and all the necessary details are up-to-date. This means making sure all the information is correct so there are no surprises later on. Examine your policy closely to un-

153

derstand what is covered and what is not. This includes understanding the amount you will have to pay before the insurance starts to cover (this is called a deductible), the amount you will pay each time you use the service (called a co-payment), and the most amount of money you will have to pay in a year (known as out-of-pocket maximum). Keeping an eye on these details will help you use your insurance policy successfully.

2. Stay In-Network

Making sure to stay "in-network" is a simple way to avoid paying extra when you visit the doctor or undergo a procedure. This means that you need to use the doctors and facilities that are approved by your insurance company. Before you have any kind of procedure, including surgery, always check that everyone involved in your care — like the hospital, the surgeon, the person who reads your X-rays (radiologist), and the doctor who gives you anesthesia (anesthesiologist) — is "in-network". This way, you won't be caught off guard by high bills afterwards. It's a small step that can save you a lot of money.

3. **Checking HSA or FSA Balances**

   Your Health Savings Account (HSA) or Flexible Spending Account (FSA) can be a financial cushion during this time. Check the balances in these accounts and understand the eligible expenses to plan your budget effectively.

4. **Pre-Authorization for the Procedure**

   Before you have a medical procedure, it is important to get pre-approval or pre-authorization from your insurance company. This means you need to contact them ahead of time to make sure they will cover the costs. It's important to understand the details: some procedures are meant to be done on an outpatient basis, meaning you go home the same day, and the insurance company may not agree to cover the costs if you stay overnight in the hospital. Also, there might be an option to have health care services provided at your home, but this also needs pre-approval. Make sure to plan ahead and know exactly what is covered to avoid any issues or unexpected bills.

5. **Discussing the Procedure with Your Doctor**

   Have an in-depth discussion with your doctor about the procedure to understand what to expect. Discuss potential costs and any preparatory actions you need to take on your end.

6. **Contact a Patient Advocate**

   Consider reaching out to a patient advocate at your insurance company. They can guide you through the process, helping you understand how to maximize your benefits while minimizing costs.

7. **Financial Counseling**

   If your hospital offers financial counseling, take advantage of this service. They can help you understand the full extent of the costs involved and discuss payment options.

8. **Budgeting for Miscellaneous Expenses**

   Apart from the procedure itself, you may incur other costs, such as transportation and post-operative care supplies. Budget for these to avoid stress later on.

9. **Setting Up a Support System**

   Before and after your procedure, it is very important to set up a team of family and friends who can help you. Many times, people may think it is better for someone who had a surgery to stay at a care facility, but actually, there are rules that may not allow this. So, it is important to talk to your family, friends, and even check with your insurance company to ensure you can have the support you need at home.

10. Physical and Mental Preparation

Prepare yourself physically and mentally for the procedure. Following your doctor's advice regarding diet and medication is critical during this time. Mental preparation, including alleviating anxieties and setting realistic expectations, is equally important.

11. Emergency Contact and Medical History

It is crucial to keep your emergency contact information current in the hospital's records. In addition, maintaining a detailed, and accessible record of your medical history is highly beneficial. Remember to list all your medications, as some may not be compatible with others. Furthermore, always inform the medical staff about any known allergies. This proactive approach helps prevent potential complications.

Preparing for a known upcoming medical procedure is a complicated process involving careful planning and coordination. Following the above steps will help provide a structured pathway to navigate this period, ensuring that every dollar is spent wisely. Remember to lean on available resources, like a patient advocate, and to maintain open lines of communication with your healthcare providers to facilitate a smooth, stress-free preparation process.

About the Author

Howard E. Deihl, RHU, possesses an extensive career spanning over three decades in the employee benefits market. His professional journey began with tenures at two general agencies in the Dallas area, which provided a strong foundation for his subsequent entrepreneurial venture. In 1999, he established his own General Agency, demonstrating leadership and vision in his field.

Holding the professional designation of Registered Health Underwriter (RHU), Mr. Deihl has illustrated a profound understanding of the industry's complexities. His accomplishments have been acknowledged by his peers with multiple awards from the National Association of Health Underwriters, reflecting a standard of excellence that he consistently upholds.

Prior to his entry into the insurance sector, Mr. Deihl honorably served in the US Army as a flight medic, assigned to a MAST unit (Military Assistance to Safety and Traffic). In this critical role, he specialized in the rescue of critically injured patients, both civilian and military, requiring skill, precision, and empathy.

Mr. Deihl's combined experiences in the military and the insurance industry have shaped his professional ethos, marked by integrity, dedication, and an unwavering commitment to excellence. His leadership and contributions to the field continue to set a benchmark in the employee benefits market, establishing him as a respected and influential figure within the industry.

Special Thanks

I am truly thankful to Taylor Weatherford, whose modeling added a special touch to this book. Fondly termed my 'supermodel', Taylor's professionalism and grace brought this book cover to life.